Reference Sources in Social Work

AN ANNOTATED BIBLIOGRAPHY

by
James H. Conrad

THE SCARECROW PRESS, INC.
Metuchen, N.J., & London
1982

Library of Congress Cataloging in Publication Data

Conrad, James H.
  Reference sources in social work.

  Includes indexes.
  1. Social service--Abstracts.   I. Title
HV 40. C66   016. 3613   81-21219
ISBN 0-8108-1503-6   AACR2

TABLE OF CONTENTS

iii

PREFACE

This bibliography brings together the major reference sources in the field of social work. Practitioners and educators, as well as librarians, should find the bibliography useful in locating information on programs, organizations, individuals, services, laws, legislation, readings, concepts, and treatment techniques.

The entries fall into two broad categories--sources in social work proper and those in allied disciplines. The former refer to the literature whose value is primarily limited to social service professionals. From this body of material--which is substantial and has grown significantly over the past decade--I have tried to compile a comprehensive list of information sources.

However, the reference materials appearing in this bibliography are not restricted to social work. Many areas of concentration in the field are shared by the behavioral and life sciences. A complete listing of reference books must therefore include some relevant works selected from the disciplines of sociology, psychology, psychiatry, health care, public administration, criminology, political science, and economics. Because of the diversity and size of the allied literature, I have of necessity restricted coverage to general and representative materials.

With the exception of historical monographs (Section 2) I have limited myself to including reference works only. There are several excellent books that treat the nonreference literature; the most recent is by Margaret B. Matson and Sheldon R. Gelman, Building the Undergraduate Social Work Library: An Annotated Bibliography (Council on Social Work Education, 1980).

The cutoff date for inclusion in the bibliography is early 1981. In order to emphasize current developments in the field I have generally omitted sources published prior to 1970, except for certain outstanding or unique books. In addition, I have attempted to select only works that are commercially available and that are likely to be found in an academic research library.

Because of the frequent changes made in social service agencies, programs, and addresses, directories often become quickly out of date. With a few exceptions, therefore, I have cited only directories that were published after 1974 or that are still available serially.

I have included many government publications, but the list is not exhaustive. Unless otherwise noted, all government publications are assumed to be obtainable from the U.S. Government Printing Office, Washington, D.C. The Superintendent of Documents stock number or classification number appears whenever possible.

In classifying the entries, I have broken the literature into six basic sections, and a number of subsections. (The choice of section and subsection headings was based on those used in the Social Work Research and Abstracts.) Within the subcategories, the citations are grouped according to format: abstracts and indexes, bibliographies, dictionaries, directories, encyclopedias, guides, handbooks, manuals, standards, and so on. Some of the entries fall into two or more subcategories. For example, a bibliography on the mental health of handicapped children might logically have been placed under the headings of mental health, child welfare, and the handicapped. These types of entries have been, in some cases, listed twice under appropriate subheadings. Nevertheless, for effective use of this bibliography, it will be necessary to consult the subject index when seeking a specialized or narrowly defined area of interest.

I did most of the research for this work at the East Texas State University Library, Commerce. In addition to the ETSU Library and various libraries in the Dallas-Fort Worth area, including the University of Texas at Arlington Social Work Collection, I found the resources of the University of Texas Perry-Castañeda Library and the Texas State Department of Human Resources Library especially valuable. Finally, I wish to extend my grateful thanks and appreciation to Robin Moore, Linda MacDonald, and Mary Lou Estes for their able assistance in typing and editing this bibliography.

REFERENCE SOURCES IN SOCIAL WORK

An Annotated Bibliography

1. GENERAL

Abstracts

1. Dissertation Abstracts International. Ann Arbor, Mich.:
   University Microfilms International, 1938- . Monthly.
   Dissertation Abstracts provides a monthly compilation of
   titles of doctoral dissertations submitted to University Microfilms by cooperating colleges and universities. Author and
   subject indexes accompany each issue and cumulate annually
   in Dissertation Abstracts International. Section A, Humanities and Social Sciences, includes three principal subject
   areas of interest to social workers: Social Work, Sociology,
   and Urban Planning. Section B, The Sciences and Engineer-
   ing, includes Health Sciences and Psychology. Computer
   searches can be made through the DATRIX (Direct Access to
   Reference Information: A Xerox Service) system.

2. Social Work Research and Abstracts. New York: National Association of Social Workers, 1965- . Quarterly.
   This indispensable source is an expansion of NASW Abstracts
   for Social Work. The volume has two main sections: the
   first part consists of original research articles in the
   field of social work and the second part consists of
   classified abstracts of over 250 professional journals
   in the social and behavioral sciences. All abstracts
   are cross-referenced. Annual author and subject indexes apear in the winter issue. Abstracts of recent doctoral dissertations (originally published annually in the Social
   Service Review from 1954 through 1974) now appear in
   SWRA's fall issue.

Indexes

3. Cumulative Index: Abstracts for Social Workers, 1965-1974.
   Edited by Inez L. Sperr. Washington, D.C.: National
   Association of Social Workers, 1977. 118p.
   Patterned on the annual index to Abstracts for Social Workers,
   this volume indexes all abstracts in ASW over a ten-year period, from Spring 1965 through Winter 1974. Citations are to
   volume number, issue number, year of publication, and abstract number.

4. Current Contents: Social and Behavioral Sciences. Philadelphia:
   Institute for Scientific Information, 1969- . Weekly.
   Current Contents reproduces the contents pages from the
   most recent issues of more than 1,250 social science journals, including many in social work, sociology, and psychology. In the back of each issue is a subject index of the significant words from the titles of the journal articles.

5. Current Index to Journals in Education (CIJE). Phoenix: Oryx,
   1969- . Monthly, with annual cumulation.
   Complementing and supplementing Resources in Education
   (item 12) and Education Index, CIJE is a selective index to
   educational materials in over 700 journals. Separate subject
   and author indexes refer users to the annotated main entry
   section. CIJE is available online.

6. Index to U.S. Government Periodicals. Chicago: Infordate
   International, 1974- . Quarterly.
   This index analyzes the contents of 150 of the most important
   government periodicals. Many of these are published by the
   Department of Health and Human Services. Arrangement is
   by author and subject.

7. KWIC (Key-Word-in-Context) Index: Publications of the National
   Conference on Social Welfare. Edited by Joe R. Hoffer.
   Columbus, Ohio: National Conference on Social Welfare,
   1964. 161p.
   Articles and publications listed are accessed through the
   KWIC index and author index. It serves mainly as an index
   to the Proceedings of the National Conference on Social Wel-
   fare (entitled The Social Welfare Forum since 1948).

8. Monthly Catalog of U.S. Government Documents. Washington,
   D.C.: U.S. Government Printing Office, 1894- .
   Monthly, with annual cumulation. GP3.8:981/1.
   The Monthly Catalog is an index to most publications issued
   by the U.S. government, including Congress and executive
   departments and branches, such as the Department of Health
   and Human Resources, HUD, and the Department of Education. It is published monthly with author, title, and subject
   indexes that cumulate annually. The Monthly Catalog is now
   available for online computer searching.

9. National Information Center for Educational Media. NICEM
   Media Indexes. Los Angeles: University of Southern
   California, National Information Center, 1967-1980.
   This service provides listings for 16mm films, 35mm filmstrips, audiotapes, videotapes, records, 8mm motion car-
   tridges, overhead transparencies, and slides. Although designed for the school media center, the entries can be useful to social workers. Indexing is by subject and title.

10. Public Affairs Information Service Bulletin. New York: Public
    Affairs Information Service, 1915- . Semimonthly.

PAIS is a subject index to publications on issues of public policy and of current social and political interest in the social sciences, business, law, education, and social work. With emphasis on statistical information, it covers books, journal articles, government documents, and the reports of public and private organizations. A Cumulative Subject Index covers the years 1915-1974. Computer searching has been available since 1976. PAIS selectively indexes books, pamphlets, government publications, and periodicals relating to social service, social work, economics, and statistical information. Indexing is by subject only.

11. Readers' Guide to Periodical Literature. New York: H. W. Wilson, 1905- . Semimonthly.
Readers' Guide indexes about 180 periodicals of general interest. Coverage includes public welfare, health care, current events, psychology, and aging. Arrangement is alphabetical by author and subject.

12. Resources in Education (RIE). Washington, D. C.: Educational Resources Information Center/Oryx, 1966- . Monthly.
Published monthly with semiannual cumulations, RIE is the companion volume to Current Index to Journals in Education (item 5) in the ERIC system. RIE indexes books, documents, reports, proceedings, papers, and curriculum material by subject, author, and sponsoring institution. Abstracts are provided for all the articles listed, and approximately 80% of the articles are available on microfiche. RIE can be computer searched. Subject areas covered pertinent to social work include the handicapped, mental health and mental retardation, social services in the schools, and social work education.

13. Social Sciences Citation Index. Philadelphia: Institute for Scientific Information, 1973- . Triannual, with annual cumulation.
The Citation Index is divided into three sections: the first provides chronological listing of cited authors and those who have cited the article; the second major element is the citing of authors and articles, under which are listed all the references contained in each article. Finally, there is a permuterm index that allows for a subject approach to the entries. The service indexes more than 1,000 ranking periodicals in areas of interest to social workers, such as community health, demography, psychology, psychiatry, sociology, urban planning, and social work.

14. Social Sciences Index. New York: H. W. Wilson, 1974- . Quarterly, with annual cumulation.
The service indexes more than 260 periodicals in social work, sociology, anthropology, archaeology, economics, and political science. Arrangement is by author and subject with numerous cross-references. The Social Sciences Index began as Readers' Guide to Periodical Literature

Supplement in 1907, was published as International Index
from 1916 to 1965, changed titles to Social Sciences and
Humanities Index in 1965, and split into Social Sciences
Index and Humanities Index in 1974.

Bibliographies and Bibliographical Guides

15. Building a Social Work Library: A Guide to the Selection of
Books, Periodicals and Reference Tools. New York:
Council on Social Work Education, 1962. 105p.
Although now dated, this bibliography has broad coverage
of the whole body of professional literature with references
from related disciplines.

16. Butler, Evelyn. "Social Welfare Libraries and Collections."
Encyclopedia of Library and Information Science, Vol.
28, pp. 95-103. New York: Dekker, 1980.
Butler's essay surveys the history of social work librar-
ianship and concludes with a bibliography.

17. Freides, Thelma. Literature and Bibliography of the Social
Sciences. New York: Bowker, 1974. 284p.
This book discusses the organization of the social sciences
as well as the literature of sociology, anthropology, psychology, and other areas related to social welfare. The
entries are annotated.

18. Gelman, Sheldon, compiler. Toward Building the Undergraduate Social Work Library: An Annotated Bibliography.
New York: Council on Social Work Education, 1971.
39p.
Though somewhat dated, Gelman's annotated bibliography
includes some 180 books that should be in the undergraduate social work library. The emphasis is on sources
to support instruction and research. The appendix lists
periodicals in the field. This book supplements item 15.

19. Gotsick, Priscilla, and others. Information for Everyday Survival: What You Need and Where to Get It. Chicago:
American Library Association, 1976. 403p.
Written for the layperson, this directory lists books, pamphlets, and articles on everyday problems. Each entry
has six columns: title (item), annotation, reading level,
physical format, source, and approximate cost. Sections
of particular interest to social workers include aging,
children, community, family, and health. With detailed
subject index.

20. Kumedan, B. S. Social Work Library: A List of Books, Periodicals and Serials. Delhi, India: University of Delhi,
School of Social Work, 1978. 139p.

Kumedan has compiled a comprehensive list of books and periodicals suitable for a large social work library.

21. Markle, Allan, and Roger C. Rinn. Author's Guide to Journals in Psychology, Psychiatry and Social Work. New York: Haworth, 1977. 256p.
This publication is designed for "scholars seeking information on the kinds of articles published by journals in the field of social work, psychology, and psychiatry." Included for each journal is information on title, address, major content areas, types of articles accepted, topics preferred, subscription cost, publication lag, review period, acceptance rate, style, style requirements, circulation, and reprint policy. With subject, title, and keyword indexes.

22. Musgrave, Gerald. Social Security Worldwide: A Classified Bibliography. Monticello, Ill.: Council of Planning Librarians, 1978. 26p.
The bibliography cites books, articles, and reports on social security systems. All the items are in English.

23. Recent Publications in the Social and Behavioral Sciences: The ABS Guide Supplement. Beverly Hills, Calif.: Sage, 1966- . Irregular.
Interdisciplinary, highly selective, and international in scope, the ABS Guide contains annotated citations to all the social and behavioral sciences. There are title and subject indexes.

24. Sheppard, Judy, compiler. Social Work Reference Aids in the University of Toronto Libraries. Toronto: University of Toronto Library, Reference Series, 1974. 100p.
All the 238 books were taken from the card catalog of the Robarts Research Library of the University of Toronto. Statistics and documents published by the government are excluded. Each item is accompanied by its LC call number. The items selected were published between 1960 and 1973.

25. Thompson, Judy L. Information Systems for Social Services: An Annotated Bibliography. Monticello, Ill.: Council of Planning Libraries, 1977. 11p.
The annotated bibliography lists books and articles on information systems for the social services. The entries are subdivided into design and planning, techniques and and tools, and applications.

26. White, Carl M. Sources of Information in the Social Sciences: A Guide to the Literature. Chicago: American Library Association, 1973. 702p.
First published in 1964, this comprehensive survey of the literature of the social sciences provides substantial an-

notated lists of reference works in the areas of psychology, sociology, and social work. Each chapter is divided into two sections: one describing the discipline, its evaluation, and direction of research, the other listing the basic reference sources. The social work section is found under the general heading of Sociology.

27. World Bibliography of Social Security. Geneva: International Social Security Association, 1963-. Quarterly.
This international quarterly provides a guide to literature and selected articles on social security, social insurance, family benefit schemes, and public assistance.

Bibliography of Bibliographies

28. Bibliographic Index: A Cumulative Bibliography of Bibliographies. New York: H. W. Wilson, 1937-. Triannual.
This is a comprehensive guide to bibliographies about numerous subjects, persons, and places. To be indexed, a bibliography must contain more than fifty items.

Dictionaries

29. Clegg, Joan. Dictionary of Social Services: Policy and Practice. 2nd ed. London: Bedford Square, 1977. 136p.
Written from a British viewpoint, the dictionary defines terms, phrases, and concepts in social work, public administration of welfare services, and related fields.

30. Makar, Ragai N., compiler. Acronyms for Social Workers. Social Work Bibliographic Bulletin #3. Garden City, N. Y.: Adelphi University Library, 1974. 35p.
Makar has compiled over 400 acronyms of social programs, organizations, government agencies, and national associations in the field of social work. For each acronym the author gives the meaning and, if an organization, when the organization was established and its location. Definitions of terms and phrases in sociology are included.

31. Wolman, Benjamin B., compiler and editor. Dictionary of Behavioral Sciences. New York: Van Nostrand Reinhold, 1973. 478p.
This comprehensive dictionary defines a variety of terms in psychology, psychiatry, psychoanalysis, neurology, psychopharmacology, endocrinology, social work, and related disciplines. It includes short biographies of psychologists, psychiatrists, and behavioral scientists. Appendixes include the American Psychiatric Association's Classification of Mental Disorders and Ethical Standards of Psychologists.

Directories

32. Barkas, J. L. The Help Book. New York: Scribner, 1979.
      667p.
      Designed for the individual citizen in need of help, this is
      a guide for finding information for 52 broad areas, such
      as health, family, counseling, education, women's issues,
      and aging. Each chapter has an introductory statement
      and annotated list of organizations with name, address,
      brief description, services provided, literature provided,
      and literature available. At the end of each chapter is a
      bibliography.

33. Catalog of Federal Domestic Assistance. Washington, D. C. :
      U. S. Office of Management and Budget, 1971- . Semi-
      annual. PrEx2.20.
      Prepared by the Office of Management and Budget, the
      catalog is a comprehensive list of all domestic programs
      involving federal grants and financial assistance adminis-
      tered by federal agencies. The entries explain the nature
      and purpose of programs, eligibility requirements, printed
      material available, and how to apply for assistance.

34. Computer-Readable Bibliographic Data Bases--A Directory and
      Data Sourcebook. Washington, D. C. : American Society
      for Information Science, 1976- . Biennial.
      This book contains information on over 500 bibliographic-
      related data bases produced in the United States and Europe.
      Some of these are of interest to social workers and social
      work related professions. Each listing includes name of
      data base, producer, distributor, generator, availability,
      size, frequency, scope, subject matter, type of material
      covered, correspondence with hard copy, publications,
      search center services, and user aids.

35. Croner, Helga, and Kurt J. Guggenheimer, compilers. Na-
      tional Directory of Private Social Agencies: A Loose-
      leaf Directory of Private Social Agencies in the United
      States. Queens Village, N. Y. : Social Service Publica-
      tions, 1964- . Annual with monthly supplements.
      A list of some 10,000 private welfare agencies providing
      direct help and referral services to individuals, this loose-
      leaf directory is classified by services offered. Part 1
      lists agencies by field of service; Part 2 is a geographic
      listing by states and cities, with address and description
      of services. The notebook is kept up to date by monthly
      supplements.

36. Directory of Affiliated Lutheran Social Service Agencies. Min-
      neapolis: Lutheran Social Service System, 1977. 80p.
      This publication covers health and welfare services for
      individuals and groups, supported partly or wholly by the
      Lutheran Church.

37. Directory of Agencies: U. S. Voluntary, International Voluntary, Intergovernmental. Washington, D. C.: National Association of Social Workers, 1973-. Annual.
First published in 1973, the directory lists more than 300 national voluntary organizations, international voluntary organizations, and intergovernmental organizations related to social work and social service. Included are notes on purpose, activities, publications, membership, officers, date of founding, address of each agency, and telephone (if in the U. S.). Some of the entries describing purpose and activities are very detailed. Foundations involved in social service are included. Agencies are listed alphabetically by agency title, and there is a subject index.

38. Directory of Diocesan Agencies of Catholic Charities in the United States, Puerto Rico, and Canada. 1979/80 ed. Washington, D. C.: National Conference of Catholic Charities, 1979. 69p. Biennial.
This biennial directory contains a list of over 600 local Catholic charity agencies and schools of social work. Entries include organization name, address, phone, and name of director.

39. Directory of Jewish Federations, Welfare Funds, Community Councils. New York: Council of Jewish Federations and Welfare Funds, 1936- . Annual.
This directory lists 230 Jewish federations, welfare funds, and community councils in the United States and Canada. Organized geographically, the entries include name, address, phone, date of founding, and name of president and executive director.

40. Directory of Jewish Health and Welfare Agencies. New York: Council of Jewish Federations and Welfare Funds, 1952- . Irregular.
This directory lists Jewish health and welfare agencies in the United States and Canada. For each agency information includes name, address, phone, and name of president.

41. Directory of Social and Health Agencies of New York City. New York: Columbia University Press, 1883- . Biennial.
First published in 1883, the 62nd compilation of social work agencies in New York City contains information on some 1,000 health and welfare agencies operating in or with headquarters in New York City. Organized alphabetically by function, each entry includes information on eligibility requirements, personnel, fees, hours, addresses, and telephone numbers. With agency index, lists selected information and referral services in the U. S. and Canada and directories of use to social workers, and personnel and subject indexes.

42. Directory of Special Libraries and Information Centers. Detroit: Gale, 1963- . Irregular.
      The 1981 edition covers 15,000 special libraries. Social work, public welfare, juvenile deliquency, and sociology libraries are included, with data on name of library, address, collection, staff, hours, etc. Of particular interest to social workers is Appendix B: Regional and Subregional Libraries for the Blind and Physically Handicapped.

43. Ethridge, James M., editor. The Directory of Directories. Detroit: Gale, 1980. 722p.
      The directory covers a wide range of publications. The entries are arranged in 15 subject categories, including Public Affairs and Social Concerns, Health and Medicine, and Social Services and Humanities. Information on each publication consists of entry number, title, publisher, address and telephone, number of listings/publications, arrangement, indexes, pages, frequency, editor, underlying concept, former title, and price.

44. Federation of Protestant Welfare Agencies Directory: A Manual for Donors and Their Advisors. Edited by Ruth A. Logan. 7th ed. New York: Federation of Protestant Welfare Agencies, 1976. 116p.
      Updated irregularly, this directory covers agencies and institutions funded by the Federation of Protestant Welfare Agencies. For each agency descriptions include details about services, size of staff, executive director, address, and telephone numbers.

45. Haimes, Norma, compiler and editor. Helping Others: A Guide to Selected Social Service Agencies and Occupations. New York: Day, 1974. 208p.
      Data for this book were collected from 650 private, federal, and state agencies during the period from September 1971 to April 1972. There are two indexes, a bibliography of directories and career guides, and a list periodicals concerned with information about social service occupations.

46. International Directory of Local United Way Organizations. Alexandria, Va.: United Way of America, 1980. 120p. Annual.
      The directory lists all local United Way funds and councils in the United States and throughout the world.

47. Klein, Bernard, editor. Guide to American Directories. Coral Springs, Fla.: Klein, 1954- . Title varies.
      This directory covers more than 6,000 directories in more than 300 major categories. Each list gives publisher's name and address, price of directory, and frequency of publication. Some of the major sections of interest to social workers are women's affairs, aging, medicine, health and welfare, psychology, and psychiatry.

48. NASW Directory of Professional Social Workers. Washington,
    D. C. : National Association of Social Workers, 1962-.
    Irregular.
    The alphabetical directory lists about 55,000 members, giv-
    ing for each person professional position, address, highest
    educational degree, and NASW affiliation.

49. National Directory of State Agencies. Washington, D. C. : In-
    formation Resources, 1974/75- . Biennial.
    This directory is a guide to over 9,000 state welfare and
    social agencies. The agencies are arranged in 93 functional
    categories, such as aging, human rights, delinquency, and
    social services, for all 50 states, the District of Columbia,
    and U. S. possessions and territories. Information on each
    agency includes the name of the bureau or division and
    overall agency, name of administrator, address, and tele-
    phone number.

50. The Public Welfare Directory. Chicago: American Public Wel-
    fare Association, 1940- . Annual.
    This directory lists all federal, state, and local public wel-
    fare agencies in the United States and Canada. The section
    on federal agencies describes their organization, adminis-
    tration, and programs. For each state there is indicated
    which agencies take administrative responsibility for public
    welfare, where to write for information on assistance, birth
    and death records, and mental health and correctional in-
    stitutions. Also included are the addresses of related state
    agencies and the directors and addresses for all county de-
    partments of social services. The appendix has a table on
    state residence requirements for assistance.

51. Service Directory of National Voluntary Health and Social Wel-
    fare. New York: National Assembly of National Volun-
    tary Health and Social Welfare Organizations, 1951-.
    Annual.
    This annotated directory describes the purposes, programs,
    services, and organizational structures of over 100 govern-
    ment and voluntary organizations affiliated with the National
    Social Welfare Assembly.

52. Ulrich's International Periodicals Directory. New York: Bow-
    ker, 11th ed. , 1965/66- . Biennial.
    Ulrich's is a comprehensive directory to periodicals and
    directories published throughout the world. Classified by
    subject, sections cover social services and welfare, chil-
    dren and youth, medical sciences, ethnic interest, psycho-
    logy, psychiatry and neurology, drug abuse and alcoholism,
    the deaf, criminology and law enforcement, sociology, etc.
    Entries include name of publication, Dewey Decimal Clas-
    sification number, country code and ISSN, subtitle, language
    of text, first year published, frequency, subscription price,
    sponsoring organization, publisher, editor, regular features,

indexes, circulation, format, and former title.

53. Washington Information Directory. Washington, D. C. : Con-
      gressional Quarterly, 1974/75- . Biennial.
      Similar to the U. S. Government Manual (item 62), this direc-
      tory contains three sections: agencies of the executive
      branch, organization of Congress, and private or "non-
      governmental" organizations. Brief descriptions of each
      are provided. Subject index, agency and organization in-
      dex, and appendixes conclude the work.

Encyclopedias

54. Encyclopedia of Associations. Detroit: Gale, 1955- . Annual.
      This annotated directory lists over 13,271 active organiza-
      tions in 18 subject categories, including social work. Vol-
      ume 2 rearranges the material by Geographic and Executive
      Index; Volume 3 updates the information. It lists the date
      the association was founded, number of staff members, a
      brief description of the association's goals and services,
      publications, annual meetings, address, telephone number,
      and executive director.

55. Encyclopedia of Social Work. 17th ed. New York: National
      Association of Social Workers, 1977. 2 vols. 1,702p.
      The encyclopedia, successor to the Social Work Yearbook,
      provides up-to-date information about all aspects of social
      work and welfare programs in the United States and Canada.
      Cross-referenced and with extensive bibliographic references,
      the 17th edition contains 192 signed articles, 106 biographies
      of social work leaders, and 54 statistical tables on demo-
      graphic and social welfare trends. Most of the articles
      have annotated bibliographies. The Social Work Yearbook
      was issued biennially from 1929 to 1951 and thereafter to
      the 14th and last edition of the Yearbook, every three years.
      The Yearbook listed international, national, and Canadian
      agencies, giving name, date of founding, address, chief
      officer, membership purpose and activities, and publications
      of each organization. A Statistical Summary (1980) updates
      the tables contained in the 17th edition of the Encyclopedia
      of Social Work.

56. The Encyclopedia of U. S. Government Benefits: A Complete,
      Practical, and Convenient Guide to United States Govern-
      ment Benefits Available to the People of America. Edited
      by Roy A. Grisham, Jr. , and Paul D. McConaughy.
      2nd ed. Union City, N. J. : Wise, 1976. 1,013p.
      Designed for the layperson, this annotated book provides
      complete coverage of over 5,000 government benefits to in-
      dividuals, and groups--ranging from social security, low-
      income housing, and Medicare to talking books for the blind.

57. Encyclopedia of U. S. Government Benefits. Coral Springs,
    Fla.: Klein, 1979. 102p.
    Prepared by a group of government experts, this is an an-
    notated encyclopedia of benefits and services available from
    the federal government.

58. International Encyclopedia of the Social Sciences. Edited by
    David L. Sills. New York: Macmillan and Free Press,
    1968. 17 vols.
    This comprehensive encyclopedia written by 1500 scholars
    attempts to summarize the state of the arts in the social
    sciences (as of 1968). In addition to articles on various
    aspects of the social sciences, the volumes contain biogra-
    phies of some six hundred persons who have contributed
    significantly to the social sciences. The 17th volume has
    a detailed subject index together with an alphabetical and
    classified list of articles. The encyclopedia includes author-
    itative articles on many aspects of social service, social
    work, psychology, psychiatry, etc. This work supplements
    its predecessor: Encyclopedia of the Social Sciences (Cro-
    well, Collier, and Macmillan, 1937, 8 vols.).

59. Social Service Organizations. Edited by Peter Romanofsky.
    Westport, Conn.: Greenwood, 1978. 2 vols. 843p.
    This lengthy encyclopedia surveys nearly 200 national and
    international social service organizations located in the
    United States. The criteria for selection of the agencies
    were historical significance, longevity, size, influence,
    presence of prominent individuals, and representativeness.
    The entries treat the history of these organizations and in-
    clude bibliographical statements. There are four separate
    indexes: organizations listed by religious affiliation, organ-
    izations listed by year of founding, organizations listed by
    agency function, and organizations listed by name change.

Manuals

60. Foster, Harold D. Disaster Planning: The Preservation of
    Life and Property. New York: Springer-Verlag, 1980.
    275p.
    Foster gives practical suggestions for disaster planning and
    preparation. Chapters are: Comprehensive Planning, Develop-
    ment and the Spatial Distribution, Safety by Design, Predict-
    ing and Preventing Disaster, Disaster Warning Systems,
    Disaster Plans, and Construction and Reconstruction.

61. Skeet, Muriel. Manual for Disaster Relief Work. London and
    New York: Churchill Livingstone, 1977. 412p.
    The author, Chief Nurse of the British Red Cross, has col-
    lected relevant information on all aspects of disaster relief
    work from disaster preparedness to selection and training
    of personnel. There are illustrations, diagrams, a glossary,
    photographs, a bibliography, and 11 appendixes.

62. United States Government Manual. Washington, D.C.: Office
of the National Register, 1935- . Annual. GS4.109.
This annual describes the purposes and programs of the
government agencies of the legislative, executive, and judicial branches of the federal government as well as the
many commissions, boards, and committees. The information listed includes the agency address and current officials
together with organizations and activities.

Proceedings

63. The Social Welfare Forum. New York: Columbia University
Press, 1873- . Annual.
These are the official proceedings of the annual forum of
the National Conference on Social Welfare. Representative
selections from among the papers and speeches are included
in these annual volumes. These papers represent the state
of the art at the time of publication.

Register

64. Federal Register. Washington, D.C.: U. S. Government Printing
Office, 1936- . Weekly.
The register contains rules and regulations of federal departments and agencies. Issues of the Register have four
sections: presidential documents, rules and regulations,
proposed rules, and notes of general interest. A modification of these rules is found in the Code of Federal Regulations, also published by the U. S. Government Printing
Office. See also The Federal Register: What It Is and
How to Use It: A Guide for the User of the Federal Register, Washington, D.C.: Office of the Federal Register,
1980, S/N 022-003-01040-6.

Statistics

65. American Statistics Index: A Comprehensive Guide and Index
to the Statistical Publications of the U. S. Government.
Washington, D.C.: Congressional Information Service,
1973- . Annual Supplements.
An excellent source on social statistics, the ASI provides
a comprehensive subject index on demographic data, vital
and health statistics, labor and social conditions, etc. Entries are annotated and contain full bibliographic data.
Monthly supplements keep the index updated. There are
subject, personal name, and corporate name indexes. Arrangement is in two parts: Part 1 indexes statistical information by subjects and names, by categories (geographic,
economic, and demographic), by title, and by agency report
numbers. Each entry provides an accession number to

Part II, the Abstracts section which provides a detailed description of the publication.

66. Statistical Abstracts of the United States. Washington, D. C. : Bureau of the Census, 1879- . Annual. C3.143.
The statistical abstract summarizes statistics on social, political, and economic characteristics of the United States under 34 broad sections. The source of the statistical data is given at the foot of each table. Statistical data are supplied by agencies of the U. S. government and by private agencies. A detailed index, arranged by subject, name, and profession, is provided.

67. Statistical Reference Index: A Selective Guide to American Statistical Publications from Sources Other Than the U. S. Government. Washington, D. C. : Congressional Information Service, 1980- . Monthly, with annual cumulation.
A supplement and complement to item 66, this publication provides the most important index to statistics on social conditions, government, politics, population, finance, and business from selected U. S. sources other than the federal government.

68. Statistics Sources: A Subject Guide to Data on Industrial Business, Social, Educational, Financial, and Other Topics for the United States and Internationally. 5th ed. Detroit: Gale, 1977. 976p.
International in scope with emphasis on the United States, this bibliography cites over 20,000 sources on nearly 12,000 subjects. The statistics cover national rather than local or regional areas.

Union Lists

69. U. S. Department of Health, Education and Welfare. Author/Title Catalogue of the Department Library. Boston: Hall, 1965. 29 vols.
A retrospective bibliography, the Author/Title Catalogue contains over 750,000 catalog cards of a major collection of material on all aspects of social work and social welfare. This multivolume set includes works located in the libraries of the U. S. Children's Bureau, the American Printing House for the Blind, Gallaudet College, and HEW.

70. U. S. Department of Health, Education and Welfare. Subject Catalogue of the Department Library. Boston: Hall, 1965. 20 vols.
The companion volume to item 69, this union list contains 350,000 LC catalog cards of books; pamphlets; papers; federal, state, and local documents; and serial publications. The entries are arranged in a straight alphabetical sequence.

71. U. S. Department of Housing and Urban Development. <u>Diction-
ary Catalog.</u> Boston: Hall, 1972. 19 vols.
This author, title, and subject catalog provides a comprehensive list of books, pamphlets, slides, films, microforms,
government publications, and research reports to HUD Library collection on urban affairs and community development. This multivolume set contains LC cards for all entries.

Yearbook and Data Book

72. <u>Municipal Yearbook.</u> Chicago: International City Managers
Association, 1924- . Annual.
The subtitle of this publication is "The Authoritative Source
Book of Urban Data and Developments." The book is or-
ganized into seven major sections: Future City, Trends,
Functions and Structure, Public Services, Municipal Activi-
ties, Directories, and References. Section E-1 summarizes
current developments in social welfare.

73. U. S. Bureau of the Census. <u>County and City Data Book.</u> Washington, D. C.: U. S. Government Printing Office, 1949- .
Irregular. S/N 0324-00121 (1972).
The <u>Data Book</u>, which is published approximately every five
years, provides statistics on population, housing, schools,
hospitals, etc., of counties and cities having more than
25,000 in population. All statistics are based on the U. S.
censuses of agriculture, business, governments, housing,
manufacturers, mineral industries, and population.

2. HISTORY OF SOCIAL WORK

Abstracts

74. America: History and Life: A Guide to Periodical Literature.
Santa Barbara, Calif.: American Bibliographic Center of
ABC-Clio, 1964- . Quarterly, with annual cumulation.
AHL abstracts and indexes journal articles on the history
and culture of U.S. from prehistoric times to the present.
Summaries of articles are grouped by subject in six major
sections with each major section divided into appropriate
subsections. Abstracts on social work history are listed
under U.S.A. 1945 to Present. Part B is an index to book
reviews, and Part C is a classified bibliography. Each
issue has subject and author indexes.

Guide

75. Descriptive Inventories of Collections in the Social Welfare
History Archives Center. Westport, Conn.: Greenwood,
1970. 846p.
Published by the Social Welfare History Archives Center of
the University of Minnesota, this volume reproduces 24 inventories of its collections. Each inventory contains a brief
history of the donor's association and a statement about the
overall organization of the collection.

Historical Statistics

76. Historical Statistics of the United States, Colonial Times to
1970. Washington, D.C.: U.S. Bureau of the Census,
1976. 2 vols. S/N003-024-00120-9.
Intended as a supplement to Statistical Abstracts (item 66), this
set provides an overview of United States history in about 12,500
statistical tables.

Monographs

77. Addams, Jane. Twenty Years at Hull House. New York:
Macmillan, 1961. 320p.
Reprint of the 1910 edition, the book recounts Addams's ex-

periences during her first 20 years at the Chicago Settlement House.

78. Axinn, June, and Herman Levin. Social Welfare: A History of the American Response to Need. New York: Dodd, Mead, 1975. 319p.
This history details the development of the American social welfare system from colonial times to the early 1970s. Each chapter contains an appendix consisting of two or three documents to illustrate the text of the chapter.

79. Bremner, Robert H. American Philanthropy. Chicago: University of Chicago Press, 1960. 230p.
The volume traces America's private and public philanthropic tradition and institutions from almshouses to U.S. participation in the United Nations.

80. Bremner, Robert H., compiler. American Social History Since 1860. New York: Appleton-Century-Crofts, 1971. 126p.
A Goldentree bibliography in American history, this classified bibliography touches on such topics as family, children and youth, minorities, social classes, reform philanthropy, delinquency, and social work. The entries are not annotated; there is an author index. See also American Social History Before 1860 (Appleton-Century-Crofts).

81. Bremner, Robert H., editor. Children and Youth in America: A Documentary History. Cambridge, Mass.: Harvard University Press, 1970 and 1974. 3 vols.
A multivolume collection of original sources and documents, this work traces the history of public policy toward children in America from the 17th century to the 20th century. It provides comprehensive coverage of the development of health, education, and welfare services for children and youth.

82. Bremner, Robert H. From the Depths. New York: New York University Press, 1956. 364p.
Broadly conceived and scholarly, the book focuses on private charities in the late 19th and early 20th centuries.

83. Bremner, Robert H. The Public Good: Philanthropy and Welfare in the Civil War Era. New York: Knopf, 1980. 234p.
Bremner traces the effects of the Civil War on American philanthropy and public welfare.

84. Breul, Frank R., and Steven J. Diner, editors. Compassion and Responsibility: Readings in the History of Social Welfare Policy in the United States. Chicago: University of Chicago Press, 1980. 372p.
Reprinted in this volume were 23 articles that originally appeared in the Social Service Review between 1929 and 1977. The editors have added biographical sketches of the

authors, bibliographical listings, and introductions to each
section. The book is divided into three sections: General
Concepts in Social Welfare History, Social Welfare in Colonial Times and the Early National Period, and Late Nine-
teenth Century Reform and Early Twentieth Century Social
Welfare Programs. The book is intended as a textbook for
use in schools of social work.

85. Bruno, Frank J., and Louis Towley. Trends in Social Work,
1874-1956. 2nd edition. New York: Columbia University Press, 1957. 462p.
The authors have prepared a history of social work based
on the proceedings of the National Conference of Social Work.
The chapters have footnotes, but there is no bibliography.

86. Cohen, Nathan Edward. Social Work in the American Tradition.
New York: Holt, Rinehart and Winston, 1965. 404p.
Cohen, former Dean of the School of Applied Social Sciences
at Western Reserve University, has written a comprehensive
history of American social work with emphasis on the Great
Depression and after. A selected bibliography is included.

87. Coll, Blanche D. Perspectives in Public Welfare: A History.
Washington, D.C.: U.S. Government Printing Office,
1969. 107p. FS17.2:P4613
This brief work traces the history of public welfare from
Elizabethan poor laws to the Great Society. Coll prepared
the history for the Intramural Research Division of the U.S.
Social and Rehabilitation Service.

88. Davis, Lenwood G. A History of Black Self-Help Organizations
and Institutions in the United States, 1776-1976: A Working Bibliography. Monticello, Ill.: Council of Planning
Librarians, 1977. 14p.
This bibliography is in three parts: Books, General Reference Works, and Black Periodicals.

89. Filler, Louis. Dictionary of American Social Reforms. New
York: Philosophical Library, 1963. 854p.
Dictionary identifies important reformers, social crusades,
reform movements, and institutions. Unfortunately there
are no bibliographical references to the definitions. Greenwood reprinted the volume in 1974.

90. Freidel, Frank, editor. Harvard Guide to American History.
Rev. ed. Cambridge, Mass.: Belknap Press of Harvard
University Press, 1974. 2 vols.
This standard bibliography covers the basic primary sources
and secondary accounts for the study of American history.
Entries on social welfare history are found under the head-
ings of Demography and Social Structure, Marriage and the
Family, Immigration and Ethnicity, and Social Ills and Re-
form.

91. Gottesfeld, Mary L., and Mary E. Pharis. Profiles in Social
    Work. New York: Human Sciences, 1977. 238p.
    The authors have interviewed seven outstanding leaders in
    the field of social work and reproduced excerpts from these
    interviews in the book. The chapter on Jane Addams has
    been derived largely from her own books and articles.

92. Klebaner, Benjamin J. Public Poor Relief in America, 1790-
    1860. New York: Arno, 1976. 253p.
    This is a reprint of Klebaner's 1951 Ph.D. dissertation sub-
    mitted to the faculty of political science at Columbia Univer-
    sity.

93. Komisar, Lucy. Down and Out in the U.S.A.: A History of
    Public Welfare. New York: New Viewpoints, 1977.
    235p.
    Written by a journalist with experience in New York City's
    antipoverty program, Down and Out is a critical history of
    American public welfare.

94. Leiby, James. History of Social Welfare and Social Work in
    the United States. Irvington, N.Y.: Columbia University
    Press, 1978.
    Leiby has prepared a useful survey of the issues, legislation,
    and events that have shaped American social welfare pro-
    grams and the profession of social work.

95. Lubove, Roy. The Professional Altruist: The Emergence of
    Social Work as a Career, 1880-1930. Cambridge, Mass.:
    Harvard University Press, 1965. 291p.
    Lubove describes the emergence of social work as a profes-
    sion.

96. Martinez-Brawley, Emilia E. Pioneer Efforts in Rural Social
    Welfare: Firsthand Views Since 1908. University Park:
    Pennsylvania State University Press, 1980. 463p.
    Eighty classic or representative statements are included,
    covering the period 1908-1940. Joanne Mermelstein and
    Paul Sundet have written an epilogue for the period since
    1940.

97. Mencher, Samuel. Poor Law to Poverty Program: Economic
    Security Policy in Britain and the United States. Pitts-
    burgh: University of Pittsburgh Press, 1974. 476p.
    Mencher traces the historical and philosophical background
    of welfare in Britain and the United States. Extensive bib-
    liographical notes conclude the monograph.

98. Remick, Cecile P. An Annotated Bibliography of Works on
    Juvenile Delinquency in America and Britain in the Nine-
    teenth Century. Norwood, Pa.: Norwood, 1976. 64p.
    This is an annotated bibliography on 19th-century juvenile
    delinquincy and juvenile corrections.

99. Ross, Edyth L., editor. <u>Black Heritage in Social Welfare,</u>
    <u>1860-1930.</u> Metuchen, N. J.: Scarecrow, 1978. 488p.
    This is a collection of unpublished documentary sources on
    black individuals and groups who initiated or supported so-
    cial service programs. The editor has prepared a nar-
    rative linkage for the documents. There is an author and
    subject index to the volume.

100. Rothman, David J. <u>Conscience and Convenience: The Asylum</u>
    <u>and Its Alternatives in Progressive America.</u> Boston:
    Little, Brown, 1980. 404p.
    Rothman explains the Progressive's approach to the depen-
    dent and deviant population and traces the emergence of
    new social institutions such as the juvenile court, proba-
    tion and parole, rehabilitation prisons, and treatment facil-
    ities for the mentally ill.

101. Rothman, David J. <u>The Discovery of the Asylums: Social</u>
    <u>Order and Disorder in the New Republic.</u> Boston:
    Little, Brown, 1971. 376p.
    In this pioneering study Rothman explains the rise of the
    asylum as a new form of social control during the Jack-
    sonian period.

102. Trattner, Walter I. <u>From Poor Law to Welfare State: A</u>
    <u>History of Social Welfare in America.</u> Riverside, N. J.:
    <u>Free Press, 1977.</u> 276p.
    This volume surveys 300 years of welfare history from
    the Elizabethan poor laws to the Charity Organization Move-
    ment (COM) through the welfare issues of the early 1970s.
    There are bibliographies at the end of each chapter but
    no footnotes.

103. Wisner, Elizabeth. <u>Social Welfare in the South: From Colon-</u>
    <u>ial Times to World War I.</u> Baton Rouge: Louisiana
    <u>State University, 1970.</u> 154p.
    Wisner provides selective coverage of welfare and social
    reform in the South. The most complete chapter is the
    one on New Orleans.

104. Zimbalist, Sidney E. <u>Historic Themes and Landmarks in So-</u>
    <u>cial Welfare Research.</u> New York: Harper & Row,
    <u>1977.</u> 432p.
    Zimbalist discusses six themes in social work research
    from the late 1800's to the present. Excerpts from some
    of the important landmark works are reproduced in the
    volume. The six major research areas discussed are
    Causes of Poverty, Measurement of the Prevalence of
    Poverty, the Social Survey Movement, Quantification and
    Indexes in Social Work, Evaluation Research on Social
    Service Effectiveness, and Study of the Multiproblem Fam-
    ily.

3. ALLIED FIELDS

A. PSYCHIATRY AND PSYCHOLOGY

Abstracts

105. Psychological Abstracts (PA). Arlington, Va.: American Psychological Association, 1927- . Monthly, with semiannual cumulation.

    The major tool for locating materials in psychology, this service abstracts over 950 journals, reports, and monographs in psychology and related disciplines, including the social services profession. Arrangement is under broad subdivision. Listings include such topics as alcohol rehabilitation, marriage and family, social structure and social roles, social psychology, clinical psychology, social casework, and counseling. Cumulative author and subject indexes have been separately published by G. K. Hall for 1927-1960. Records since 1967 are available on machine-readable tapes and provide the basis for the automated search and retrieval service known as Psychological Abstracts Information Service (Psych INFO).

Bibliography

106. Markle, Allan, and Roger C. Rinn, editors. Author's Guide to Journals in Psychology, Psychiatry, and Social Work. New York: Haworth, 1977. 256p.

    This guide was designed for authors desiring to submit manuscripts for consideration in the field of psychology, psychiatry, and social work. The journals are arranged alphabetically, with information on review period, acceptance ratio, manuscript preference areas, where the journal is indexed or abstracted, circulation, and other data about the journal itself. There are three indexes: subject, title, and keyword.

Dictionaries

107. American Psychiatric Association. A Psychiatric Glossary: The Meaning of Terms Frequently Used in Psychiatry. 5th ed. Waltham, Mass.: Little, Brown, 1980. 152p.

This dictionary supplies authoritative definitions of 1,500 terms used in psychiatry. Terms have been cross-referenced and are arranged in both alphabetical order and according to subject. It also lists drugs used in psychiatry, commonly abused drugs, legal and research terms, neurologic defects, schools of psychiatry, and psychological tests.

108. Hinsie, Leland E., and Robert J. Campbell. Psychiatric Dictionary. 4th ed. New York: Oxford University Press, 1973. 816p.
The authors give definitions and illustrative quotations of words and concepts in the field of psychiatry.

109. LaPlanche, Jean. Language of Psycho-analysis. New York: Norton, 1974. 510p.
This dictionary defines terms and concepts used in psychoanalysis. Each entry discusses historical, structural, and problematic aspects of the term or concept. Essays on major terms are often several pages in length and include bibliographies.

Directories

110. Directory of Certified Psychiatrists and Neurologists. Chicago: Marquis, 1979- . Irregular.
This publication provides a list of over 14,500 certified psychiatrists and neurologists. For each psychiatrist or neurologist entries include name, office address, phone, educational and career data, memberships, and teaching position.

111. Directory of Counseling Services. Washington, D.C.: International Association of Counseling Services, 1950- . Annual.
This directory contains information on fees, hours, types of counseling services, methods of counseling, and location of 385 accredited counseling services in the United States. All agencies included are either accredited or provisional members of the American Personnel and Guidance Association (APGA).

Encyclopedias

112. Eysenck, Hans Jurgen, editor. Encyclopedia of Psychology. New York: Herder and Herder, 1972. 3 vols.
This international encyclopedia contains about 500 articles on terms, concepts, and theories of psychology. Although most articles are short definitions of terms, 284 topics have been selected for extended discussion. These contain bibliographies for further readings. Included, also,

are biographies of psychologists and psychiatrists who have
made important contributions to the discipline. In 1979
the Seabury Press published an unabridged one-volume reprint of the three-volume work; the entries have not been
updated in this new volume.

113. Goldenson, Robert M. The Encyclopedia of Human Behavior:
      Psychology, Psychiatry, and Mental Health. Garden
      City, N.Y.: Doubleday, 1970. 2 vols.
      This encyclopedia surveys the entire spectrum of mental
      health, psychology, and psychiatry. The 1,000 entries
      range from short essays on terms to long essays on con-
      cepts, theories, and treatment techniques often supported
      by case histories. There are two indexes, one analytical
      and the other categorical. Brief biographies of famous
      psychiatrists and psychologists are included.

114. Klein, Barry T. Reference Encyclopedia of American Psy-
      chology and Psychiatry. Rye, N.Y.: Todd, 1975.
      459p.
      Entries describe a wide spectrum of associations, societies,
      organizations, research centers, special libraries, founda-
      tions, mental health centers, psychology graduate schools,
      psychiatric training programs, periodicals, and audiovisual
      aids. Most entries are briefly annotated. A subject-
      category index breaks down all listings into 30 fields of
      study.

115. Wolman, Benjamin B., editor. International Encyclopedia of
      Psychiatry, Psychology, Psychoanalysis, and Neurology.
      New York: Van Nostrand Reinhold, 1977. 12 vols.
      Some 2,000 authorities took seven years to complete this
      overview of psychology, psychiatry, psychoanalysis, and
      neurology. All problems of mental health and disorder,
      as well as their diagnostic and treatment methods, are
      included. Length of articles ranges from one paragraph
      to over 30 pages. The work contains biographic sketches
      of famous men and women in the disciplines of psychology,
      psychiatry, and neurology. The final volume contains a
      list of articles represented, a name index, and a subject
      index.

116. Wright, Logan, and others. Encyclopedia of Pediatric Psy-
      chology. Baltimore: University Park Press, 1979. 933p.
      The encyclopedia presents short essays on 114 topics in
      the field of medical psychology for children. Each entry
      includes citations to relevant research. Some of the topics
      surveyed give an indication of the coverage: abortion,
      battered children, behavior therapy, cerebral palsy, drug
      abuse, suicide, tongue thrusting, and obesity. Supplemen-
      tary materials include a term glossary, a test glossary,
      and an exhaustive list of references.

Handbooks

117. Arieti, Silvano, editor. American Handbook of Psychiatry.
2nd ed. Revised. New York: Basic Books, 1975.
6 vols.
Written by recognized experts in the field of psychiatry,
this multivolume work covers all prominent viewpoints.
The six volumes are: Foundations of Psychiatry; Child,
Adolescent, Sociocultural and Community Psychiatry; Adult
Clinical Psychiatry; Organic Disorders and Psychosomatic
Medicine; Treatment; and New Frontiers. Each volume has
subject and name indexes.

118. Nicholi, Armand M., Jr., editor. The Harvard Guide to
Modern Psychiatry. Cambridge, Mass.: Harvard University Press, 1978. 691p.
Written by recognized authorities in the field of psychiatry,
this book is arranged in six parts: Examination and Evaluation, Brain and Behavior, Psychopathology, Principles
of Treatment and Management, Special Populations, and
Psychiatry and Society. All chapters have bibliographies
and lists of recommended readings.

Tests

119. Buros, Oscar K., editor. The Mental Measurements Yearbook. Highland Park, N.J.: Gryphon, 1938-1972. 7
vols.
These seven volumes can help social workers to locate,
evaluate, and use standardized tests. Each edition supplements earlier ones by listing new editions of tests and
new articles discussing the tests.

120. Buros, Oscar K., editor. Personality Tests and Reviews:
Including an Index to the Mental Measurements Yearbook. Highland Park, N.J.: Gryphon, 1970.
1,659p.
Personality Tests and Reviews is a comprehensive guide
to personality tests in the first six Mental Measurements
Yearbooks.

121. Buros, Oscar K., editor. Tests in Print II: An Index to
Tests, Test Reviews, and the Literature on Specific Tests. Highland Park, N.J.: Gryphon, 1974.
1,107p.
Buros has compiled a bibliography of separately published
tests in print. Title, personal name, and classified
indexes, as well as a directory of publishers, are
included.

B. SOCIOLOGY AND ANTHROPOLOGY

Abstracts

122. <u>Sociological Abstracts</u>. La Jolla, Calif.: Sociological Abstracts, 1953- . Five issues per year.
This service identifies and abstracts more than 150 sociological journals and secures abstracts from an additional
400 social science journals. The abstracts are arranged
according to broad professional interest, e. g., poverty,
family and socialization, social psychiatry, social gerontology, social service, and philanthropy. The abstracts are
complete. The data base of <u>Sociological Abstracts</u> is available for searching through the Lockheed/DIALOG system.

Bibliographies

123. <u>Annual Review of Sociology</u>. Palo Alto, Calif.: Annual Reviews, 1975- . Annual.
This review seeks to present, in summary form, current
research in sociology. The reviews are written by specialists and include bibliographical references. Volume 5 in
the series contains a cumulative index of authors and chapter titles for Volumes 1-5.

124. Harzfeld, Lois A. <u>Periodical Indexes in the Social Sciences
and Humanities: A Subject Guide</u>. Metuchen, N. J.:
Scarecrow, 1978. 174p.
The author has compiled an annotated guide to abstracting
and indexing serial publications in the humanities and social sciences. The book has a comprehensive index and
many cross-references.

125. <u>International Bibliography of Sociology</u>. Chicago: Aldine,
1952- . Annual.
Compiled by the International Committee for Social Docu-
mentation, this bibliographical service annually includes
3,000 to 5,000 entries for books, articles, reports, and
book reviews, arranged under broad subject headings.
Social service, social work, social problems, family, and
ethnic groups are treated as separate categories in the
bibliography. Alphabetical indexes of authors and of subjects are given in the back. The first four volumes of
the bibliography were published in issues of <u>Current So-
ciology</u>, 1951-1954.

126. Sussman, Marvin B. <u>Author's Guide to Journals in Sociology
and Related Fields</u>. New York: Haworth, 1978. 214p.
Sussman supplies detailed information for publishing scholars in the field of sociology and related areas, including
social work. Other guides relevant to social work include
<u>Author's Guide to Journals in the Health Field</u> and <u>Author's
Guide to Journals in Law, Criminal Justice and Criminology</u>.

Dictionaries

127. Hoult, Thomas Ford. Dictionary of Modern Sociology. To-
     towa, N. J.: Littlefield, Adams, 1969. 408p.
     This dictionary defines terms and concepts in sociology
     and related disciplines and illustrates many of the defini-
     tions with quotations from sociological literature.

128. Mitchell, G. D. A Dictionary of Sociology. Chicago: Aldine,
     1968. 224p.
     This dictionary defines over 1,100 concepts and theories
     in sociology. Most of the longer entries are signed and
     contain bibliographies. Also included are biographical
     sketches of deceased sociologists.

129. Winick, Charles, editor. Dictionary of Anthropology. New
     York: Greenwood, 1969. 578p.
     A reprint of the 1956 edition, this work defines some
     8,000 technical and common terms and concepts for both
     physical and cultural anthropology.

Encyclopedia

130. Hunter, David E., and Phillip Whitten, editors. Encyclopedia
     of Anthropology. New York: Harper & Row, 1976.
     411p.
     Articles cover terms, theories, and trends in anthropology.
     There are maps, diagrams, photographs, and other illus-
     trative materials.

Shelflist

131. Sociology, Widener Library Shelflist, No. 45 and 46. Cambridge,
     Mass.: Harvard University Library: distr. Harvard
     University, 1973. 2 vols.
     This shelflist contains approximately 49,000 titles of books,
     pamphlets, and periodicals on sociological history, theory,
     social groups, social problems, social psychology, and
     social welfare. The second volume is an author and title
     index. Each entry has full bibliographic data.

C.   ECONOMICS

Index

132. Business Periodicals Index. New York: H. W. Wilson,
     1958-   . Monthly.

Business Periodicals Index is a cumulative subject index to over 270 English-language periodicals in the fields of business, economics, accounting, banking, labor, taxation, etc. Cost of welfare, government spending on health and human services, the economy, and unemployment are just some of topics of interest to social workers.

Bibliography

133. Daniells, Lorna M. Business Information Sources. Berkeley: University of California Press, 1976. 439p.
A revision of Edwin T. Coman's Sources of Business Information (2nd ed., University of California Press, 1964), this bibliography covers business, statistical sources, financial information, real estate, insurance, accounting, management, personnel, marketing, sales, foreign trade, and basic industries.

Dictionaries

134. Abraham, Samuel V. Real Estate Dictionary and Reference Guide. Orange, Calif.: Career, 1979. 309p.
The first part of the dictionary defines terms and concepts used in real estate. The second part gives statistics, tables, and directory-type information.

135. Ammer, Christine, and Dean S. Ammer. Dictionary of Business and Economics. New York: Free Press, 1977. 461p.
Prepared for both the layperson and specialist, this dictionary consists of definitions and explanations of more than 3,000 terms, concepts, and theories in economics and business. The definitions are supported by charts, tables, and diagrams.

136. Greenwald, Douglas, and others. McGraw-Hill Dictionary of Modern Economics: A Handbook of Terms and Organizations. 2nd ed. New York: McGraw-Hill, 1973. 792p.
First published in 1965, this work defines some 1,400 terms and concepts used in economic theory and applied economics. It contains descriptions of approximately 225 private, public, and nonprofit agencies active in the field of business and economics. This book should be used in conjunction with the Encyclopedia of Banking and Finance (item 144).

137. Kohler, Eric L. A Dictionary for Accountants. 5th ed. Englewood Cliffs, N.J.: Prentice-Hall, 1975. 497p.
Kohler defines some 3,000 terms, concepts, and abbreviations.

138. Moffat, Donald W. Economics Dictionary. New York: Elsevier, 1976. 301p.
This standard work defines terms and concepts for the fields of economics, finance, banking, labor, business, and government. The appendix includes a five-page listing of abbreviations and a number of charts and graphs.

139. Moore, Norman D. Dictionary of Business, Finance and Investment. New York: Investor's System, 1975.
This general dictionary of basic terms in finance and banking includes definitions that vary in length from ten words to ten pages.

140. Sloan, Harold S., and Arnold J. Zurcher. Dictionary of Economics. 5th ed. New York: Barnes & Noble, 1970. 520p.
This dictionary identifies approximately 3,000 agencies, court decisions, legislative acts, theories, and concepts pertaining to economics.

Directories

141. Kruzas, Anthony T., and Robert C. Thomas, editors. Business Organizations and Agencies Directory. Detroit: Gale, 1980. 894p.
Although not an all-inclusive directory, this is an excellent source for locating information on chambers of commerce; better business bureaus; commercial businesses; business-related associations; stock-exchanges; federal, state, and regional agencies; trade fairs; conventions and conferences; franchise companies; hotel/motel systems; etc. Also included are publishers, data banks, information centers, business libraries, research centers, and educational institutions.

142. Poor's Register of Corporations, Directors, and Executives. New York: Standard and Poor, 1928- . Annual.
This publication lists alphabetically some 34,000 U.S. and Canadian Corporations with names of officials, products manufactured, and number of employees.

143. Who's Who in Finance and Industry. Chicago: Marquis, 1936- . Biennial.
This directory contains biographical information on some 18,500 businessmen and women from large, medium, and small firms.

Encyclopedia

144. Munn, Glenn G., editor. Encyclopedia of Banking and Finance. 7th ed. Rev. and enl. Boston: Bankers, 1973. 953p.

This standard reference work includes information on
money, credit, government regulations, economics, and
other matters relating to banking and finance. Bibliographies and charts are included. The first edition of the
encyclopedia was published in 1924.

Desk Book

145. Institute for Business Planning. Real Estate Desk Book. 5th
ed. Englewood Cliffs, N. J.: Prentice-Hall, 1977.
529p.
This work covers all aspects of real estate: mortgages,
closings, zoning laws, trusts, condominiums, title search
requirements, etc.

Maps

146. Oxford Regional Economic Atlas: The United States and Canada. 2nd ed. London: Oxford University Press,
1975. 128p.
This work is an economic atlas that includes 128 pages of
maps.

147. Rand McNally Commercial Atlas and Marketing Guide. Chicago: Rand McNally, 1876- . Annual.
The Rand McNally Commercial Atlas provides extensive
coverage for the United States. Double-page maps show
information on retail sales, manufacturing, and other aspects of business. There are statistical tables and an
exhaustive index.

Statistics

148. Market Guide. New York: Editor and Publisher, 1924- .
Annual.
This work provides statistical data for some 1,500 American and Canadian cities. Statistics can be found on population, climate, industries, department stores and chain
stores, banks, colleges and universities, newspaper circulation, etc.

149. U. S. Bureau of Labor Statistics. Handbook of Labor Statistics. Washington, D. C.: U. S. Government Printing
Office, 1926- . Annual. L2. 3:2000.
This annual includes over 160 tables on wages and salaries,
prices, unemployment, social security, health care costs,
and other subjects relating to labor.

D. POLITICAL SCIENCE

Bibliographies and Bibliographic Guides

150. McCarrick, Earlean M. U.S. Constitution: A Guide to In-
        formation Sources. Detroit: Gale, 1980. 390p.
        This is the fourth volume in a series of 13 existing and
        planned works in Gale's American Government and History
        Information Guide Series. The guide covers the history
        of the Constitution, the amendments to the Constitution,
        and the Constitution itself.

151. Vose, Clement. A Guide to Library Sources in Political
        Science: American Government. Washington, D.C.:
        American Political Science Association, 1975. 135p.
        This is a well-written, detailed guide to sources in the
        field of political science. Unfortunately it does not have
        an index.

152. Wilson, David E. National Planning in the United States: An
        Annotated Bibliography. Boulder, Colo.: Westview,
        1979. 279p.
        This annotated bibliography on planning contains 2,000 en-
        tries. Chapters have introductory narrative and several
        are subdivided.

Dictionaries

153. Plano, Jack C., and Milton Greenberg. The American Politi-
        cal Dictionary. 4th ed. New York: Holt, Rinehart
        and Winston, 1979. 488p.
        This standard work gives concise definitions of about 1,200
        terms, agencies, court cases, and statutes on all aspects
        of American political life from the local to the national
        level. It is organized into 18 topical chapters. There is
        a general index to all the entries.

154. Safire, William. Safire's Political Dictionary: An Enlarged
        Up-to-Date Edition of "The New Language of Politics."
        New York: Random House, 1978. 845p.
        Designed for the layperson and the politician, this new
        edition of Safire's dictionary contains terms and phrases
        relating to American politics and current events.

155. Smith, Edward, and Arnold J. Zurcher, editors. Dictionary
        of American Politics. 2nd ed. New York: Barnes,
        1968. 434p.
        Although some of the information is dated, this dictionary
        includes some 4,500 terms, government agencies, and
        legistiative acts of significance in American politics and
        law.

Directories

156. Taylors' Encyclopedia of Government Officials: Federal and
        State. Westfield, N. J.: Political Research, 1967- .
        Annual, with monthly and quarterly updates.
        This reference work gives biographical information for
        25,000 state and federal officials. Current information
        on officials is available via a "hot line" telephone service.

157. U. S. Congress. Official Congressional Directory for the Use
        of the U. S. Congress. Washington, D. C.: U. S. Govern-
        ment Printing Office, 1809- . Biennial. Y4. P93/1:1/9.
        This directory offers information on the United States Con-
        gress: biographical data on members of Congress, mem-
        bership on congressional committees and boards, and list
        of administrative and legislative assistants with home ad-
        dresses. Additional information is available on the Execu-
        tive and Judicial branches and the U. S. diplomatic corps.

158. Who's Who in American Politics. New York: Bowker, 1967- .
        Biennial.
        This directory consists of biographical data on the presi-
        dent and other federal, state, and local officials, elected and
        appointed.

Guide

159. Congressional Quarterly's Guide to Congress. 2nd ed. Wash-
        ington, D. C.: Congressional Quarterly, 1976. 719p.
        This reference work provides detailed information on the
        operation of the U. S. Congress.

Almanacs

160. Almanac of American Politics. New York: Dutton, 1972- .
        Biennial.
        This almanac contains information on the political situation,
        economic base, ethnic and religious makeup of voters,
        recent election results, etc., for each state and congres-
        sional district. Biographical data and ratings by various
        interest groups are provided for U. S. senators and repre-
        sentatives.

161. Congressional Quarterly Almanac. Washington, D. C.: Con-
        gressional Quarterly, 1945- . Annual.
        A compilation of information contained in the Congressional
        Quarterly Weekly (item 162), this almanac has sections
        on the Congress, summary of legislation, characteristics
        of each member of Congress, and subcommittee and com-
        mittee assignments. Chapters are assigned to major areas
        of legislation for the previous year. Charts and graphs
        are included.

Reports

162. Congressional Quarterly Service Weekly Reports. Washington,
      D. C. : Congressional Quarterly, 1943- . Weekly.
      This service summarizes congressional and other govern-
      mental affairs for the previous week--new bills, progress
      of pending legislation, committee actions, voting records,
      Supreme Court actions, etc. A chart shows the progress
      of legislation through Congress, and a listing of House
      and Senate votes keyed to the Congressional Record. The
      weekly issues are indexed quarterly.

Robert's Rules

163. Robert, Henry M. Robert's Rules of Order: Newly Revised.
      New and enl. ed. , by Sarah Corbin Robert and others.
      Glenview, Ill. : Scott, Foresman, 1970. 594p.
      This first major revision of the Rules since 1915, the
      Robert's Rules is the authoritative manual of parliamentary
      procedures.

Statistics

164. Scammon, Richard M. , and Alice McGillivray, compilers and
      editors. America Votes: A Handbook of Contemporary
      American Election Statistics. Washington, D. C. : Con-
      gressional Quarterly, 1956- . Biennial.
      Arranged by state, the reference work gives election sta-
      tistics since WWII for governors and senators and the most
      recent figures for U. S. representatives.

165. U. S. Office of Management and Budget. The United States
      Budget in Brief. Washington, D. C. : U. S. Government
      Printing Office, 1950- . Annual. S/N041-001-00172-7
      (1981).
      This is an abridged version of the United States budget.
      It is less technical than the complete text: The Budget of
      of the United States Government. S/N041-001-00173-2
      (1981).

E.   URBAN AFFAIRS

Abstracts and Indexes

166. Index to Current Urban Documents. Westport, Conn. : Green-
      wood, 1971- . Quarterly.
      This index lists the official publications of the largest
      cities and counties in the United States and Canada.

167. Sage Public Administration Abstracts. Beverly Hills, Calif.:
    Sage, 1974- . Quarterly.
    This service cross-indexes abstracts on all aspects of pub-
    lic administration.

168. Sage Urban Studies Abstracts. Beverly Hills, Calif.: Sage,
    1973- . Quarterly.
    This abstracting service includes references to books,
    articles, and government publications in the field of urban
    studies.

169. Urban Affairs Abstracts. Washington, D.C.: National League
    of Cities/U.S. Conference of Mayors, 1971- . Weekly.
    This abstract monitors 800 periodicals, journals, and news-
    letters on urban affairs.

170. Urban Affairs Reporter. Chicago: Commerce Clearing House,
    1967- . Biweekly.
    This looseleaf service provides information on federal pro-
    grams affecting state and local governments.

Bibliographies and Bibliographic Guides

171. Bell, Gwendolyn, Edwina Randall, and Judith E. R. Roeder.
    Urban Environments and Human Behavior: An Anno-
    tated Bibliography. Stroudsburg, Pa.: Dowden, Hutch-
    inson & Ross, 1973. 271p.
    This bibliography is divided into three parts: Design Ap-
    proaches to the Urban Environment, Social Sciences Ap-
    proaches to Urban Environment, and Framework of the
    Urban Environment.

172. Boyce, Byrl N., and Sidney Turoff. Minority Groups and
    Housing: A Bibliography, 1950-1970. Morristown,
    N.J.: General Learning, 1972. 202p.
    The authors have compiled an annotated bibliography on
    housing minorities.

173. Darden, Joe T. The Ghetto: A Bibliography. Monticello,
    Ill.: Council of Planning Librarians, 1977. 25p.
    Selected books and articles on the ghetto are included in
    this brief annotated bibliography.

174. Directory of Federal Statistics for Local Areas: A Guide to
    Sources: Update 1977-1978. Washington, D.C.: Bu-
    reau of the Census; distr. U.S. Government Printing
    Office, 1980. S/N003-024-02167-6.
    This guide gives sources on statistics for cities and stan-
    dard metropolitan areas.

175. Hoover, Dwight W. Cities. New York: Bowker, 1976. 231p.

The author cites books, articles, films, filmstrips, and other media that discuss the past, present, and future of the American urban experience. Major subdivisions are: Ethnic Groups in the City, Housing in the City, Urban Poverty, Urban Reform and the Provision of Services, Urban Planning, and Urban Sociology. Annotations are lengthy and critical. With author and title indexes.

176. Murphy, Thomas P. Urban Politics: A Guide to Information Sources. Detroit: Gale, 1978. 248p.
This annotated bibliography covers all aspects of urban politics. Preference has been given to works published since 1970. With author and title indexes.

177. Spear, George E., and Donald Mocker, editors. Urban Education: A Guide to Information Sources. Detroit: Gale, 1978. 203p.
The authors have compiled an annotated bibliography on urban education, using monographs, journal articles, government documents, ERIC microfiche, dissertations, and reports. Other bibliographies in the Gale Urban Information Series are: Anthony Filipovitch, Urban Community (1978); Bernard H. Ross, Urban Management (1979); Ernest Alexander, Anthony J. Catanese, and David S. Sawicki, Urban Planning (1979); Dennis Palumbo, Urban Policy (1979); Thomas P. Murphy, Urban Indicators (1980); Thomas P. Murphy, Urban Law (1980); and Jean A. Shackelford, Urban and Regional Economics (1980).

178. U.S. Department of Housing and Urban Development. Dictionary Catalog of the United States Department of Housing and Urban Development, Library and Information Division, Washington, D.C. Boston: Hall, 1973. 19 vols.
This is a retrospective bibliography of the holdings of the libraries of the Federal Housing Administrations, Public Housing Administration, and the Housing and Home Finance Agency. It is kept up to date through periodical supplements.

Directories

179. Braddock's Federal-State-Local Government Directory. Washington, D.C.: Braddock, 1975- . Annual.
This directory lists federal and state government agencies and their officials plus principal officials of the nation's counties. Entries include agency name, address, phone, function, etc.

180. National Association of Regional Councils Directory. Washington, D.C.: National Association of Regional Councils, 1971- . Annual.
This directory lists approximately 670 municipal, county,

and local governmental organizations throughout the United States. For each council information includes name, address, phone, director, founding date, area population, budget, function, etc.

Encyclopedia

181. Whittick, Arnold, editor. Encyclopedia of Urban Planning. New York: McGraw-Hill, 1974. 1,218p.
International in scope, the encyclopedia contains over 400 articles by 70 leading world authorities on urban planning. Biographies of prominent planners are included as well as explanations of planning terms and techniques. Maps, illustrations, and a detailed index are useful features of the work.

Glossary

182. Abrams, Charles. The Language of Cities: A Glossary of Terms. New York: Viking, 1971. 365p.
Prepared for laypeople and professional planners and administrators, this glossary defines terms related to cities, urban planning, politics, and administration. The author was one of the world's leading urban planners and housing experts.

Handbooks

183. The Book of the State. Lexington, Ky.: Council of State Government, 1935- . Biennial.
Chapters cover Constitutions and Elections, Legislatures and Legislation, Judiciary, Administrative Organization, Finance, Intergovernmental Relations, and Major State Services. The last chapter is a listing, state by state, of major officers and statistics.

184. Brian, J. L. Berry, editor. City Classification Handbook: Methods and Applications. New York: Wiley-Interscience, 1972. 394p.
Brian presents methods of studying a city's economic, political, and social variations.

Reports

185. Urban Data Service Reports. Washington, D.C.: International City Management Association, 1969- . Monthly.
This service analyzes a different topic each month relating to urban planning and urban politics. Statistics are often included.

Yearbook

186. The Municipal Yearbook. Washington, D. C. : International
     City Management Association, 1934- . Annual.
     The chapter on urban development covers planning organi-
     zations--their nature and proliferation. Also covered are
     public safety, county government, fiscal condition, welfare
     services, etc.

4. FIELDS OF SERVICE

A. ADOPTION

Bibliographies

187. Adoption--Related Literature. Albany, N. Y.: Welfare Research, 1976. 137p.
     Intended for the professional social worker, this bibliography annotates books, articles, and unpublished material printed between 1960 and 1976 on adoption and related areas.

188. Jacka, Alan A. Adoption in Brief: Research and Other Literature in the United States, Canada and Great Britain, 1966-72: An Annotated Bibliography. Windsor, England: NFER, 1973. 71p.
     Some 236 books, articles, and research reports on adoption are annotated in this update of Adoption--Facts and Fallacies. Most of the works were published between 1965 and 1972. Entries are arranged in four sections.

189. Van Why, Elizabeth Wharton, compiler. Adoption Bibliography and Multi-Ethnic Sourcebook. Hartford: Open Door Society of Connecticut, 1977. 320p.
     This book is divided into two sections: Part 1 is the annotated bibliography of 1,250 books, articles, reports, proceedings, and audiovisual materials on adoption. Part 2 describes 130 sources for dolls, toys, games, calendars, and children's books, and tells where these items can be purchased. There are periodical and ethnic indexes.

Directory

190. American Public Welfare Association. National Directory of Inter-Country Adoption Services Resources. Washington, D. C.: Children's Bureau; distr. U. S. Government Printing Office, 1980. 212p. S/N017-091-00233-9.
     Based on a 1979 survey, this directory lists over 600 state public welfare agencies, U. S.-based international adoption groups, domestic organizations, and parent groups that give help to those interested in adopting non-U. S. children.

Handbook

191. Leavy, Morton, and Roy D. Weinberg. Law of Adoption.
     4th ed. Dobbs Ferry, N.Y.: Oceana, 1979. 117p.
     Revised by the Oceana Editorial Board, this legal almanac
     briefly summarizes all legal aspects of adoption. A glos-
     sary, appendix, and subject index are included.

Standards

192. CWLA Standards for Adoption Service. Rev. ed. New York:
     Child Welfare League of America, 1978. 101p.
     An update of the 1968 and 1973 CWLA standards for adop-
     tion, this work sets forth the basic principles for quality
     adoption services.

B. AGING AND THE AGED

Abstracts and Indexes

193. Current Literature on Aging. Washington, D.C.: National
     Council on Aging, 1957- . Quarterly.
     This service indexes selected books and periodical articles
     dealing with aging and such related topics as housing, so-
     cial welfare and community services, institutional care,
     health, and employment. Each issue contains approximately
     150 entries. All entries are annotated.

194. Research on the Mental Health of the Aging, 1960-1976. Rock-
     ville, Md.: National Institute of Mental Health, 1977.
     69p. S/N017-024-00624-6
     Prepared by the Center for Studies of the Mental Health
     of the Aging, this work abstracts basic research in geria-
     tric psychiatry and psychology of aging.

Bibliographies

195. Allyn, Mildred V., compiler. About Aging: A Catalog of
     Films, with a Special Section on Videocassettes. 4th
     ed. Los Angeles: University of Southern California,
     Ethel Percy Andus Gerontology Center, 1979. 249p.
     This is a catalog of audiovisual materials--16 mm films
     and videocassettes--on aging and the aged. The work
     lists, for each film or videocassette, the title, producer,
     length, year, whether black-and-white or color, and cost.

196. Balkema, John B., compiler. A General Bibliography on Ag-
     ing. Washington, D.C.: National Council on the Aging,
     1972. 52p.

The works cited in the bibliography were all published between 1967 and 1972.

197. Bell, Duran, and others. Delivering Services to Elderly Members of Minority Groups: A Critical Review of the Literature. Santa Monica: Calif. : Rand Corporation, 1976. 103p.
Sponsored by the U. S. Administration on Aging, the book is divided into two sections: a critical review of the literature on problems of elderly members of minority groups, followed by an extensive bibliography. The authors discuss the inadequacies of the social service delivery system to the Asian-American, Mexican-American, American Indian, and black elderly.

198. "Current Publications in Gerontology and Geriatrics," Journal of Gerontology, 1964- . Quarterly.
The Journal of Gerontology publishes in each issue a classified list of books, articles, conference papers, and official publications of interdisciplinary scope on aging. The bibliography updates and supplements Shock's Classified Bibliography on Aging.

199. Dancy, Joseph. The Black Elderly: A Guide for Practitioners with Comprehensive Bibliography. Ann Arbor, Mich. : Institute of Gerontology, 1977. 56p.
Dancy identifies and describes a wide range of resources pertaining to the black elderly in America.

200. Davis, Lenwood G. The Black Aged in the United States: An Annotated Bibliography. Westport, Conn. : Greenwood, 1980. 216p.
This is a comprehensive listing of books, dissertations, theses, government publications, and articles on the black aged in the United States. The appendixes includes a list of black old-folks' homes, 1860-1980, and a list of relevant periodical titles.

201. Regnier, Victor, and others. Mobile Services and the Elderly: A Bibliography. Monticello, Ill. : Council of Planning Librarians, 1977. 21p.
This subject bibliography is a guide to articles and reports on mobile medical services; mobile dental services; mobil social and home-delivered services; mobile coronary care units; and mobile hospital, recreational, and cultural services.

202. St. Clair, Duane. Bibliography of Social Work and Aging. Washington, D. C. : National Association of Social Workers, 1976. 45p.
St. Clair's bibliography updates Beryl Carter's Annotated Selective Bibliography for Social Work with the Aging (Council on Social Work Education, 1968).

203. Sharma, Prakash C. Aging and Communication: A Selected
     Bibliographic Research Guide: Part II (1971-1975).
     Monticello, Ill.: Vance Bibliographies, 1978. 10p.
     A continuation of Part I, this bibliography lists over 125
     works published between 1971 and 1975 on communication
     processes and the elderly. It is arranged in two sections:
     Books and Articles.

204. Sharma, Prakash C. Nursing Homes and Nursing Home Ad-
     ministration: A Selected Research Bibliography. Mon-
     ticello, Ill.: Vance Bibliographies, 1978. 8p.
     This annotated bibliography lists over 100 articles and
     books published between 1960 and 1977 on nursing homes
     and nursing home administration.

205. Sharma, Prakash C. A Selected Guide to Films on Aging.
     Monticello, Ill.: Vance Bibliographies, 1978. 11p.
     Sharma annotated 77 films and filmstrips on the sociology
     of aging. Information on each film includes title, length
     of film, mailing address, and if the film is black-and-
     white or color.

206. Sharma, Prakash C. Sociology of Retirement: A Selected
     Bibliographic Research Guide (1950-1973). Monticello,
     Ill.: Vance Bibliographies, 1978.
     Sharma's bibliography contains over 150 works published
     between 1950 and 1973 on the sociological aspects of re-
     tirement. The bibliography is arranged in two sections:
     Part 1 contains a listing of books and Part 2 is a listing
     of articles.

Directories

207. AAHA Membership Directory. Washington, D.C.: American
     Association of Homes for the Aging, 1981. 136p.
     This work was previously issued under the title Directory
     of Non-profit Homes for the Aged. The AAHA publishes
     a directory describing over 1,600 nonprofit homes, inter-
     mediate-care homes, and housing projects that belong to
     the Association, and 500 suppliers, individuals, and lawyers
     associated with AAHA.

208. Directory of Jewish Homes for Aged. Dallas: National As-
     sociation of Jewish Homes for Aged, 1962- . Irregular.
     This directory lists Jewish homes for the elderly in the
     United States and Canada. Information for each facility
     includes name, address, number of beds, admission re-
     quirements and procedures, name of administrator, and
     description of residents' characteristics.

209. A Guide for Selection of Retirement Housing. Washington,
     D.C.: National Council on the Aging, 1976. 36p.

An adaptation of an introduction to the Council's The National Directory on Housing for Older People (item 211), this brief volume outlines criteria for the selection and evaluation of nursing and retirement housing for the elderly.

210. International Meals on Wheels Directory. Washington, D.C.: National Association of Meals Programs, 1980. 100p. This annual directory describes about 1,000 programs that provide hot meals to ill or elderly persons in the United States and Canada.

211. The National Directory of Housing for Older People. Washington, D.C.: National Council on the Aging, 1965- . Irregular. This national directory of housing for the elderly gives information on type of housing, number of living units, costs, services, admission requirements, and sponsor. The NCOA is an information clearinghouse in the field of aging for senior citizens, professionals, and interested laypeople.

Factbook

212. Fact Book on Aging: A Profile of America's Older Population. Washington, D.C.: National Council on the Aging, 1978. 236p. Topics covered include demography, income, employment, physical health, mental health, housing, transportation, and criminal victimization. There is a bibliography at the end of the work.

Handbooks

213. Biegel, Leonard. The Best Years Catalogue: A Source Book for Older Americans. New York: Putnam, 1978. 224p. Biegel designed this book to help older people "find the resources to live a fuller and more productive life." Chapters cover such topics as health, transportation, travel, social services, and recreation. The catalog cites books, pamphlets, and agencies that serve older citizens.

214. Match, Sandra K. Establishing Telephone Reassurance Services. Washington, D.C.: National Council on the Aging, 1972. 21p. Prepared for the Office of Economic Opportunity by the National Council on the Aging, this handbook summarizes the general principles of quality telephone reassurance services for the aging. There is a bibliography.

215. Norback, Craig, and Peter Norback. The Older American's Handbook. New York: Van Nostrand Reinhold, 1977. 311p.

This comprehensive work covers sources of information on aging, including 168 libraries for the blind and physically handicapped; 102 federal programs that provide jobs and supplemental income; 293 books, pamphlets, and magazines about the elderly; and 64 conferences, shows, and conventions for the elderly. In addition, agencies and organizations serving the elderly are included.

216. Otten, Jane, and Florence D. Shelley. When Your Parents Grow Old: Information Resources to Help the Adult Son or Daughter Cope with the Problems of Aging. New York: Funk and Wagnalls, 1976. 298p.
Written for the layperson, the book provides information on how to deal with aging parents. Appendix A and Appendix B list agencies and organizations serving the old and retired.

217. Padula, Helen. Developing Day Care for Older People. Washington, D.C.: National Council on the Aging, 1972. 70p.
This handbook offers individuals and social agencies basic principles for establishing and operating a day-care center for senior citizens.

218. Planning and Financing Facilities for the Elderly: A Resource Handbook. Washington, D.C.: American Association of Homes for the Aging, 1977. 218p.
This volume includes an extensive bibliography and subject index.

219. Planning Housing Services for the Elderly: A Process Guidebook. Washington, D.C.: American Association of Homes for the Aging, 1977. 39p.

220. Source Book on Aging. 2nd ed. Chicago: Marquis, 1977. 539p.
Arranged in ten sections, this publication reprints government documents, studies, and statistics on aging. Names and addresses of state officials charged with administering programs for the aged, and voluntary agencies and organizations concerned with aging are listed. There are subject and geographic indexes.

Manual

221. Melemed, Brina B. Making Title XX Work: A Guide to Funding Social Services for Older People. Washington, D.C.: National Council on Aging, Title XX Assessment Project, 1976. 54p.
Prepared for social service professionals, this pamphlet covers the history of Title XX of the Social Security Act,

program goals of Title XX, federal ceilings on grants, administrative requirements, eligibility for service, and much other useful information about Title XX.

C.   ALCOHOLISM AND DRUG ABUSE

Bibliographies and Bibliographical Guides

222.   Austin, Gregory A., and others. Guide to the Drug Research Literature. Rockville, Md.: National Institute on Drug Abuse, 1979. 397p. S/N017-024-00980-6.
Designed to serve as a cumulative index to the 27 volumes of the National Institute on Drug Abuse Research Issue Series, this guide summarizes the purpose, methodology, findings, and conclusions of 1,300 sources. There are six indexes.

223.   Chalfant, H. Paul, and Brent S. Roper, compilers. Social and Behavioral Aspects of Female Alcoholism: An Annotated Bibliography. Westport, Conn.: Greenwood, 1980. 145p.
This is a comprehensive annotated bibliography on female alcoholism. The entries, all published between 1970 and 1979, are arranged into eight broad subject areas: Female Alcoholism: Comparisons, Rates, and Patterns; Psychological and Psychiatric Aspects of Female Alcoholism; Social and Cultural Aspects of Female Alcoholism; Medical and Psychical Concomitants of Female Alcoholism; Death, Suicide, Homicide, and Female Alcoholism; Families of Female Alcoholics; Treatment and Female Alcoholics; and the Alcoholic's Spouse.

224.   Drug Abuse Bibliography. Troy, N.Y.: Whitston, 1970- . Irregular.
Designed to update Joseph Meditto's Drugs of Addiction and Non-Addiction: Their Use and Abuse (1970), this bibliography provides access to research material--periodicals, books, essays, and doctoral dissertations--in the field of drug and narcotic addiction. Coverage is international in scope. Entries are arranged into over 120 subject headings.

225.   Drug Dependence and Abuse: A Selected Bibliography. Chevy Chase, Md.: National Clearinghouse for Drug Abuse Information; distr. Washington, D.C.: U.S. Government Printing Office, 1971. 51p. PrEx13.10:D84/471.

226.   Iiyama, Patti, and others. Drug Use and Abuse Among U.S. Minorities: An Annotated Bibliography. New York: Praeger, 1976. 247p.

This bibliography is organized around five racial minorities: blacks, Asian-American, Mexican-Americans, Native Americans, and Puerto Ricans. Lengthy annotations, cross-references, and name and subject indexes are provided.

227. National Clearinghouse for Alcoholism Information. In Focus: Alcohol and Alcoholism Media. Washington, D. C.: U. S. Government Printing Office, 1977. 73p. S/N017-024-00573-8.
For each item in the bibliography information is provided on title, length, color or black-and-white, distributor, sale price, rental fee, audience, year of release, and synopsis of film content. Subject and alphabetical indexes complete the work.

228. National Institute on Alcohol Abuse and Alcoholism. Alcoholism Prevention: Guide to Resources and References. Rockville, Md.: Alcohol, Drug Abuse, and Mental Health Administration, U. S. Public Health Service, 1979. 88p. HE20. 8308:Al1/5.
This volume contains abstracts of reports and periodical articles on all aspects of alcoholism and drug abuse.

229. Sandmaier, Marian. Alcohol Programs and Women: Issues, Strategies and Resources. Rockville, Md.: National Clearinghouse for Alcohol Information, 1977. 26p. HE20. 8302:W84/2/Review.
Sandmaier's volume surveys health agencies in the U. S. directly serving women alcoholics. A bibliography is included.

230. Selected Bibliography on Drugs of Abuse. Chevy Chase, Md.: National Institute of Mental Health, 1970. 25p. HE-20. 2417:D84/2.
This selected bibliography was prepared in cooperation with the U. S. Bureau of Narcotics and Dangerous Drugs.

231. Wells, Dorothy P. Drug Education: A Bibliography of Available Inexpensive Materials. Metuchen, N. J.: Scarecrow, 1972. 111p.
This bibliography is designed to be used in drug education programs. The bulk of the material in the bibliography consists of inexpensive pamphlets and ephemeral material (up to $2.50). Wells has starred the titles she feels are the most significant items. There are author, title, and subject indexes.

Dictionaries

232. Hardy, Richard E., and John G. Cull. Drug Language and Lore. Springfield, Ill.: Thomas, 1975. 171p.
Intended primarily for persons working in drug rehabilita-

tion, the directory contains more than 2,000 terms and definitions concerned with drug abuse and treatment.

233. Lingeman, Richard R. Drugs from A to Z: A Dictionary.
2nd ed. New York: McGraw-Hill, 1974. 310p.
Designed for both the layperson and the professional, the dictionary defines drug concepts, terms, and slang of drugs and drug abuse. Quotations often follow definitions to illustrate how the term is used. Most definitions are short, but many run to several pages in length. For example, the one on heroin covers seven pages.

Digest

234. The Alcoholism Digest. Rockville, Md.: Information Planning Associates, 1972/73- . Annual.
The digest contains abstracts of reports, books, serial publications, and other types of literature on alcoholism. Abstracts are arranged in six categories: general, education and research, treatment and rehabilitation, legal, social and economic aspects, and traffic safety. Author and subject index are included in each issue.

Directories

235. Alcoholism and Drug Abuse Treatment Centers Directory: A Guide to Alcoholism and Drug Abuse Treatment Centers and Services. Santa Monica, Calif.: Ready Reference, 1981. 350p.
This computer printout of U. S. drug abuse and alcoholism programs gives name, address, and phone number for each treatment center. The appendix contains a list of Veterans Administration Medical Centers.

236. Alcoholism Treatment Facilities Directory: United States and Canada. Washington, D. C.: Alcohol and Drug Problems Association of North America, 1974. 360p. Irregular.
Updated irregularly, this volume lists alcoholism treatment facilities in the United States and Canada.

237. Directory of Drug Abuse and Alcoholic Treatment Programs. Rockville, Md.: National Institute on Drug Abuse, 1976- . Irregular.
Compiled by the staff of the National Clearinghouse for Drug Abuse Information, this national directory lists over 10,000 federal, state, local, and privately funded drug abuse treatment facilities with name, address, phone, and brief description of treatment offered. The directory is kept up to date through the NCDAI, which publishes a computer printout of local treatment facilities. The NCDAI

will make telephone and written referrals to direct help.

Encyclopedia

238. High Times Encyclopedia of Recreational Drugs. New York: Stonehill, 1978. 417p.
Well illustrated and very comprehensive, this factbook covers the potential "recreational" uses and potential harm of drugs.

Handbooks

239. Bludworth, Edward. Three Hundred Most Abused Drugs. 3rd rev. ed. Tampa, Fla.: Trend House, 1976. 30p.
This pamphlet contains color photos of the 300 most-abused drugs, with name, ingredients, and level of potential abuse.

240. Dupont, Robert I., and others, editors. Handbook on Drug Abuse. Washington, D.C.: National Institute on Drug Abuse, 1979. 452p. S/N017-024-00869-9.
This handbook covers all aspects of drug abuse treatment. There is a lengthy bibliography.

241. Gold, Robert S., and William H. Zimmerli. Drugs: The Facts; A Handbook for the Helping Professionals. Dubuque, Iowa: Kendall/Hunt, 1973.
This publication identifies the most commonly abused drugs. The appendix contains journals on drugs and drug abuse, agencies involved with drug abuse programs, legal implications of possession and use of illicit drugs, glossary of drug terms, evaluation of drug abuse prevention films, and chemical structures of drugs.

242. Narcotics and Drug Abuse A to Z. Vols. 1-3. Queens Village, N.Y.: Social Service Publications, Division of Croner, 1971. Looseleaf.
This multivolume work serves as a resource guide about drug abuse. Each volume consists of five sections: 1) a compilation of terms in the field of drugs, narcotics, and drug addiction; 2) profiles of the most abused or most dangerous drugs; 3) individuals involved in drug abuse facilities and research; 4) miscellaneous; and 5) a directory of facilities and organizations.

D. CHILD ABUSE

Bibliographies

243. Eskin, Marian. Child Abuse and Neglect: A Literature Re-

view and Selected Bibliography. Washington, D. C. :
U. S. Department of Justice, National Institute of Justice, 1980. 118p. J28:11:C43.
This bibliography annotates the current literature (journals,
reports, and books) on child abuse and neglect. An overview of the literature introduces the bibliography.

244. Harris, Susan, and Joanne Bravieri, compilers. Bibliography
of Child Abuse Literature. Chicago: National Committee for Prevention of Child Abuse, 1974. 43p.
This bibliography has books and journal articles dealing
with prevention, identification, and treatment of child abuse.

245. Kalisch, Beatrice J. Child Abuse and Neglect: An Annotated
Bibliography. Westport, Conn. : Greenwood, 1978.
535p.
Kalisch has compiled and classified a bibliography of over
2,000 books, articles, reports, and government publications that deal with the legal, psychological, and medical
aspects of child abuse. The appendixes include a directory
of organizations interested in child abuse and a reprint of
the Child Abuse Prevention and Treatment Act (Public Law
93-247). There are two indexes: an author index and a
keyword subject index.

246. Polansky, Norman A. , and others. Child Neglect: An Annotated Bibliography. Washington, D. C. : Community
Services Administration, 1975. 90p. (SRS)76-23041.
This bibliography contains more than 140 books and articles
on all aspects of child abuse and neglect.

247. Wells, Dorothy P. , and Charles R. Carroll, editors. Child
Abuse: An Annotated Bibliography. Metuchen, N. J. :
Scarecrow, 1980. 450p.
This bibliography annotates books, chapters of books, journal articles, films and videocassettes, government publications, pamphlets, and dissertations relating to child abuse,
treatment of child abuse, and legislation of child abuse in
the United States.

Directories

248. Child Abuse and Neglect Programs. Washington, D. C. : National Center on Child Abuse and Neglect, 1976- .
Irregular. HE1. 480/4:976.
This directory contains descriptions of over 2,200 service-
oriented child abuse and neglect programs in the U. S.
Information on each program includes services, clientele,
staffing, organization, coordination, funding, and address.
There is a program director index, an organization index,
and a subject index.

249. National Directory of Child Abuse Services and Information.

Chicago: National Committee for Prevention of Child Abuse, 1974- . Irregular.
The National Committee for Prevention of Child Abuse publishes a directory listing child abuse programs by state, with the location, telephone number, sponsoring agency, staff, and services. This publication has been discontinued.

Glossary

250. Interdisciplinary Glossary on Child Abuse and Neglect: Legal, Medical, Social Work Terms. Washington, D. C. : National Center on Child Abuse and Neglect; distr. Washington, D. C. : U. S. Government Printing Office, 1978. 100p. S/N017-000-00206-6.
Compiled by the Midwest Parent-Child Welfare Resources Center, the glossary defines all important terms used in child abuse and related fields. Useful features are the inclusion of names and addresses of organizations involved in child abuse and a list of commonly used acronyms.

Handbooks

251. Caulfield, Barbara. Child Abuse and the Law: A Legal Primer for Social Workers. Chicago: National Committee for Prevention of Child Abuse, 1979. 64p.
In addition to presenting an introduction to child abuse laws, the book includes information on the interpretation of child abuse laws as they affect social workers.

252. Costa, Joseph J. , and Gordon K. Nelson. Child Abuse and Neglect: Legislation, Reporting, and Prevention. Lexington, Mass. : Heath, 1978. 417p.
This publication lists social agencies concerned with child abuse. Entries include name of agency and address.

253. Katz, Sanford N. , and others. Child Neglect Laws in America. Chicago: American Bar Association, 1976. 372p.
The authors discuss and define court powers in child neglect cases, role of counsel, penalities for parents judged unfit, and termination of parental rights. All the mandatory child abuse reporting acts are analyzed.

Standards

254. Burb, Robert A. , and Michael Wald. Standards Relating to Abuse and Neglect. Cambridge, Mass. : Ballinger, 1977. 191p.
This publication is part of the Juvenile Justice Standards Project of the American Bar Association.

255. Federal Standards for Child Abuse and Neglect Prevention and
     Treatment Programs and Projects. Washington, D. C.:
     Advisory Board on Child Abuse and Neglect and the
     National Center on Child Abuse and Neglect, 1978. 324p.
     Prepared by the National Institute for Advanced Studies,
     this publication epitomizes the standards for federally funded
     child abuse programs.

E. CHILD WELFARE

Abstracts

256. Child Development Abstracts and Bibliography. Chicago: So-
     ciety for Research in Child Development, 1927- .
     Triannual.
     This service is essentially an annotated bibliography of
     100 U. S. and foreign periodical articles and books relating
     to the growth and development of children. There are
     six subject areas: Biology, Health, and Medicine; Cogni-
     tion, Learning, and Perception; Social, Psychological, Cul-
     tural, and Personality Studies; Educational Processes;
     Psychiatry and Clinical Psychology; and History, Theory,
     and Methodology. The book has author and subject in-
     dexes.

257. Perkins, Barbara B. Adolescent Birth Planning and Sexuality:
     Abstracts of the Literature. New York: Child Welfare
     League of America, 1974. 75p.
     Perkins has abstracted 101 articles on teenage pregnancy,
     adolescent abortion, and adolescent sexuality.

258. The Psychoanalytic Study of the Child, Volumes 1-25: Ab-
     stracts and Index. New Haven, Conn.: Yale Univer-
     sity Press, 1975. 414p.
     The book indexes and abstracts all 516 papers appearing
     in Volumes 1-25 of the Psychoanalytic Study of the Child.
     The papers cover psychoanalytic concepts, theory building,
     and clinical studies regarding child development. A sub-
     ject index to the abstracts is included.

259. Williams, Tannis M. Infant Care: Abstracts of the Litera-
     ture--Supplement. Washington, D. C.: Consortium on
     Early Childbearing and Child Rearing, Child Welfare
     League of America, 1974. 203p.
     An update of Infant Care: Abstracts of the Literature, the
     supplement abstracts articles, papers, government reports,
     and books published mostly between 1972 and 1974. The
     entries have been arranged in five areas: Infant Develop-
     ment, Infant-Adult Relationships, Child Rearing Patterns,

Infant Education Intervention and Day Care, and Theoretical and Methodological Issues. An index precedes each section.

Bibliographies and Bibliographic Guides

260. Benson, Hazel B. Behavior Modification and the Child: An Annotated Bibliography. Westport, Conn.: Greenwood, 1979. 398p.
This classified bibliography, containing 2,309 entries, provides access to the literature on behavior modification with children. Included are books, chapters in books, journal articles, reports, and dissertations. The addendum is organized into three sections: Basic Bibliographical Tools, Audio-Visual Materials, and Glossary.

261. Berlin, Irving N., editor. Bibliography of Child Psychiatry and Child Mental Health. New York: Human Sciences, 1976. 508p.
An update of Berlin's 1963 bibliography, the volume is a reading list on child psychiatry for psychiatrists and social workers. All entries are annotated. The main section of the bibliography is followed by a selected list of films. There are subject and author indexes.

262. Bernstein, Joanne E. Books to Help Children Cope with Separation and Loss. New York: Bowker, 1977. 255p.
Bernstein prepared this list of books to help children between the ages of three and 16 cope with problems of separation and loss. There are 438 annotated books, as well an sections entitled: Selected Reading for Adult Guides, Using Books to Help Children Cope with Separation and Loss, and Bibliography.

263. Cross, Lee, and Kenneth W. Goin, editors. Identifying Handicapped Children: A Guide to Case Finding, Screening, Diagnosis, Assessment and Evaluation. New York: Walker, 1977. 127p.
Part two of this textbook contains a 62p. annotated bibliography of screening, diagnosis, and assessment instruments with information on prices and availability of listed materials.

264. Dreyer, Sharon Spredeman. Bookfinder. Circle Pines, Minn.: American Guidance Service, 1978. 2 vols.
This bibliography includes a list of 1,000 children's books designed to help children and young adolescents (2-15) cope with specific developmental needs and problems. Topics covered by the books include adoption, boy-girl relationships, divorce, fantasy, friendship, imagination, loneliness, personal appearance, prejudice, and sibling rivalry. Most of the books cited are fiction. The books are indexed by subject, author, and title.

265. Dunmore, Charlotte J. Black Children and Their Families:
     A Bibliography. San Francisco: R & E Research,
     1976. 103p.
     Dunmore has compiled 1,200 citations under eight head-
     ings: Adoption; Education; Health; Family Life; Life in
     the Ghetto; Mental Health; Sex, Contraception, and Family
     Planning; and Miscellaneous. The works were largely pub-
     lished between 1960 and 1975.

266. Garoogian, Andrew, and Rhoda Garoogian. Child Care Issues
     for Parents and Society: A Guide to Information Sour-
     ces. Detroit: Gale, 1977. 367p.
     This comprehensive work identifies and annotates books,
     audiovisual materials, government publications, and organ-
     izations dealing with child care. Arrangement of entries
     is by subject. Appendixes list children's magazines, poi-
     son control centers, and book publishers. Author, title,
     and subject indexes are included.

267. Gillis, Ruth J. Children's Books for Times of Stress: An
     Annotated Bibliography. Bloomington: Indiana Univer-
     sity Press, 1978. 322p.
     Some 250 books suitable for children between preschool
     age and third grade who face stressful situations are in-
     cluded in this annotated bibliography. Among the topics
     covered by the books are death, divorce, hospitalization,
     jealousy, and sibling rivalry.

268. Moore, Coralie B. , and Kathryn Gorham Morton. A Reader's
     Guide for Parents of Children with Mental, Physical,
     or Emotional Disabilities. Pueblo, Colo. : Consumer
     Information Center, 1976. 144p.
     An outgrowth of Selected Reading Suggestions for Parents
     of Mentally Retarded Children prepared by the Children's
     Bureau in 1967, this volume is a bibliography of books on
     how to deal with a disabled child. Disabilities listed in-
     clude mental retardation, physical handicaps, epilepsy,
     hearing impairments, cleft palate, multiple handicaps, and
     learning disabilities.

269. Shur, Janet, and Paul V. Smith. Where Do You Look? How
     Do You Know? Information Resources for Child Advo-
     cates. Washington, D. C. : Children's Defense Fund,
     1980. 128p.
     Designed to help parents, this book suggests sources of
     social data on children, such as federal documents, sur-
     veys, and statistics. The author gives information on
     federal and state programs for children. The appendix
     consists of: A Guide to Sources Cited in the Text, Se-
     lected Federal Depository Libraries, State Project Direc-
     tors for the Cooperative Health Statistics Systems, Selected
     List of Directories, and so forth.

270. Stewart, Karen Robb, compiler and editor. Adolescent Sexuality and Teenage Pregnancy: A Selected, Annotated Bibliography with Summary Forewords. Chapel Hill: Carolina Population Center, University of North Carolina, 1976. 43p.
    Eight short essays introduce a selective annotated bibliography on sexuality and teenage pregnancy.

271. Von Pfeil, Helena P. Juvenile Rights Since 1967: An Annotated, Indexed Bibliography of Selected Articles and Books. South Hackensack, N. J.: Rothman, 1974. 199p.
    This annotated bibliography contains more than 1,400 entries selected from a wide range of disciplines and countries on juvenile courts and children's rights.

272. Walker, Deborah Klein. Runaway Youth: Annotated Bibliography and Literature Overview. Technical Paper No. 1. Washington, D. C.: Office of Social Services and Human Development, 1975. 110p. (SS-HD Technical Analysis Paper No. 1.) HE1.52:1.
    Walker has written lengthy annotations of 122 articles, books, dissertations, government documents, reports, and popular magazine and newspaper articles on runaway youth. Each entry contains the author's professional background, author's definition of a runaway, composition of sampling, methodology used in the study, and major findings and recommendations of the author.

273. White, Anthony G. Runaway Youth as a Problem to the City: A Selected Bibliography. Monticello, Ill.: Council of Planning Librarians, 1975.
    White has compiled a brief bibliography on runaway youth.

Directories

274. Directory for Child Advocates. Washington, D. C.: Coalition for Children and Youth, 1977. 115p.
    The Coalition for Children and Youth is a confederation of 130 national organizations and 1,200 state and local members acting as a clearinghouse for those concerned with the welfare of children.

275. The Directory for Exceptional Children: A Listing of Educational Facilities. Boston: Porter Sargent, 1954- . Biennial.
    The 9th edition (1980) is a guide to 3,000 educational and training facilities for the mentally retarded, physically handicapped, and emotionally disturbed. Arrangement is by type of agency, with a further breakdown by states and cities. Information on the agency includes address, size of staff, cost, therapy available, and brief description of

the type of students accepted. In addition to a list of associations, societies, and foundations concerned with exceptional children, the appendix contains a partial listing of government agencies sponsoring special programs for handicapped and exceptional children.

276. Directory of Member Agencies and Associate Agencies of the Child Welfare League of America. New York: Child Welfare League of America, 1977- . Annual.
Accredited member agencies, public and private, of the Child Welfare League are listed by state along with the name of the director, the telephone numbers, and services. The introduction of the directory contains the names of the officers and members of the board of directors of the Child Welfare League and a description of the services provided by the league sponsors. There is also a statement of the requirements for accredited members. Issued in a two-volume set, the directory is revised every January.

277. International Halfway House Association--Directory of Residential Treatment Centers. Cincinnati, Ohio: The Association, 1968- . Annual.
This national directory provides a comprehensive, current reference to more than 3,500 halfway houses and centers that provide group homes and mental health services. Entries include name of program, address, phone, year established, director's name, capacity, age and sex restrictions, and primary function.

278. Johnson, Clara L., editor. Directory of Child Protective Programs and Services in the Southeastern United States. Athens, Ga.: Regional Institute of Social Welfare Research, 1979. 326p.
The author lists approximately 270 hospitals providing special child life and play programs. Each entry includes the address of the hospital, name of contact, number of beds, number of units, pediatric age range, staff, and types of programs.

279. Johnson, Laurence, and Associates. Catalog of Federal Youth Programs. Division of Youth Activities; distr. Washington, D. C.: U. S. Government Printing Office, 1977. 501p. S/N017-091-00216-9.
Compiled from the 1977 Catalog of Federal Domestic Assistance (item 33), this volume describes 160 federal programs for youth available through the federal government. Program descriptions are arranged by department. Information on each entry includes the following: title, popular name, administering agency, program number, legal basis, objectives, brief description, assistance information, elegibility requirements, application procedures, and information contact.

280. The National Children's Directory: An Organizational Direc-
     tory and Reference Guide for Changing Conditions for
     Children and Youth. College Park, Md.: Urban Infor-
     mation Interpreters, 1977. 303p.
     Over 700 organizations devoted to improving children's
     legal and social conditions are represented in this directory.
     Entries include information on address, telephone number,
     purpose, and publications. The organizations are divided
     into two separate sections: national groups are listed alpha-
     betically by name, and local groups alphabetically by state.
     Subject and agency indexes are included.

281. The National Directory of Children and Youth Services. 1980-
     82 ed. Washington, D.C.: Children Protection Report
     Directory Services, 1981. 550p.
     This directory provides key information on agencies respon-
     sible for social, health, and juvenile court/youth services.
     The directory provides key information on agencies and
     program officials in city, county, state, and federal agen-
     cies. Information on each agency includes telephone num-
     ber, address, types of service available, and names of
     administrators. The appendix contains a complete "Who's
     Who" of federal administrators governing children and
     youth programs and key staffers of Congressional commit-
     tees responsible for writing legislation affecting young
     people.

282. National Directory of Runaway Programs. Washington, D.C.:
     National Youth Work Alliance, 1979. 130p.
     This state-by-state directory describes over 200 programs
     and presents a discussion of the historical background of
     runaways. Entries for each agency include sponsor, ad-
     dress, phone, contact person, facilities, services, type
     of runaways served, and success rate.

283. U.S. Facilities and Programs for Children with Severe Men-
     tal Illnesses: 1977 Directory. 2nd ed. Rockville,
     Md.: National Institute of Mental Health and National
     Society for Autistic Children, 1977. 504p. S/N017-024-
     00689-1.
     This directory lists about 500 programs and facilities for
     children diagnosed as autistic, schizophrenic, or having
     other childhood psychoses or severe mental disorders.
     For each entry information includes capacity, fee, staff,
     admission criteria, and type of services available.

284. United States Federal Interagency Committee for the Interna-
     tional Year of the Child. Federal Programs That Re-
     late to Children, 1979. Washington, D.C.: U.S. Ad-
     ministration for Children, Youth and Families; and Se-
     cretariat, International Year of the Child, 1979. 125p.
     HE1.2:C43/5.
     This reference source is an excellent guide to federal pro-

grams for children and youth. Organized by department
and by agency, it provides a brief description of programs,
appropriations, and names of programs authorized but not
funded.

285. Youth-Serving Organizations Directory. 2nd ed. Detroit:
Gale, 1980. 1,179p.
Most of the information on the youth-serving organizations
in the directory were abstracted from the Encyclopedia of
Associations (item 54). The index is arranged in alphabetical order by the first word of the organization's name.
Information includes name of the organization, address,
telephone number, date founded, members, staff, director,
purposes, publications, committees, and convention meeting data. Data on research centers and special libraries
are also included.

Handbooks

286. Copeland, William C. Finding Federal Money for Children:
Financing Services for Children through Title XX and
Other Programs. Washington, D.C.: Child Welfare
League of America and Hecht Institute for State Child
Welfare Planning, 1976. 63p.
This pamphlet explains how to obtain Title XX funding for
children's programs. Other pamphlets on related topics
by Copeland include Manual No. Five: A Roadmap Through
Title XX (Child Welfare League of America, 1978) and
Obtaining Federal Money for Children's Services (Child
Welfare League of America, 1976).

287. Crow, Gary. Children at Risk: A Handbook of the Signs and
Symptoms of Early Childhood Difficulties. New York:
Schocken, 1978. 192p.
The author discusses symptoms and profiles of childhood
problems as well as suggestions for coping with these
problems. A bibliography and an index are included.

288. Helping in Child Protective Services: A Casework Handbook.
Englewood, Colo.: American Humane Association,
1981. 252p.
This is a step-by-step approach, in outline form, to child
protective services. Selected references, a glossary, and
an index round out the work.

289. Johnson, Orval G., and James W. Bommarito. Tests and
Measurements in Child Development: A Handbook. San
Francisco: Jossey-Bass, 1971. 518p.
This book describes psychological tests suitable for children between birth and the age of 12 with information on
the name and author of the test; the age level of the test;
a description of the test; information on variables, relia-

bility, and validity; and sources from which the measure may be obtained. All the tests included in the volume are unpublished and are not included in The Mental Measurements Yearbook (item 119).

290. Johnson, Orval G. Tests and Measurements in Child Development, Handbook II. San Francisco: Jossey-Bass, 1976. 2 vols.
A supplement and update of Handbook I (item 289), this volume provides a comprehensive guide to psychological tests for children (to age 18) and provides information on type and description of measurements. Tests and measurements are arranged in 11 broad categories. Author and subject indexes complete the work.

291. Princeton Center for Infancy and Early Childhood. Parents' Yellow Pages. Edited by Frank Caplan. Garden City, N.Y.: Anchor, 1978. 571p.
This book contains 130 articles on health care for children. Each article has an extensive bibliography and suggestions on where to find assistance.

292. Rose, Carol M. Some Emerging Issues in Legal Liability of Children's Agencies. New York: Child Welfare League of America, 1978. 68p.
This pamphlet discusses the implications of the latest judicial decisions regarding the rights of children, rights to treatment, invasion of privacy, termination of parental rights, rights of foster and adoptive parents, discrimination issues, and issues of information disclosure. It includes bibliographical references.

293. Schaefer, Charles E., and Howard L. Millman. Therapies for Children. San Francisco: Jossey-Bass, 1977. 501p.
The author has identified common behavior problems of children and located specific therapeutic techniques that others have found effective in resolving these problems. Disorders are arranged in six sections: Neurotic Behaviors, Habit Disorders, Antisocial Behaviors, Hyperkinetic Behavior, Disturbed Relationships with Children, and Disturbed Relationships with Parents. There are author and subject indexes.

294. Sloan, Irving J. Youth and the Law: Rights, Privileges and Obligations. 3rd ed. Dobbs Ferry, N.Y.: Oceana, 1978. 118p.
The book gives full coverage in the following areas of interest to social service professionals: Judicial System; Youth and Ownership and Operation of Motor Vehicles; Youth and Contracts; Youth and Law of Torts; Youth, Narcotics and Alcohol; Juveniles and Criminal Justice; Youth and Marriage; Youth and Labor Law; Youth and the School;

and Youth and the Environment. There is a glossary of
legal terms.

295. Thomas, George, and others. The Legal Status of Adolescents. Athens, Ga.: Regional Institute of Social Welfare Research, 1980. 408p.
This report discusses the laws and court decisions on adolescents for all 50 states. Minor's consent relative to
marriage, birth control and abortion, child labor laws,
and the limits of juvenile court jurisdiction are just some
of the 47 topics treated in the volume.

Manual

296. Copeland, William C. Finding Federal Money for Children's
Services. New York: Child Welfare League of America,
1976. 63p.
The volume describes sources of funding for children's
services with primary emphasis on Title XX funds. Three
other manuals--Obtaining Federal Money for Children's
Services, Managing Federal Money for Children's Services
and A Roadmap Through Title XX--complete the series.

Reviews

297. Annual Review of Child Abuse and Neglect Research. Washington, D. C.: U. S. Children's Bureau, 1976- . Annual.
HE23. 1210/3.
The Children's Bureau publishes the latest research on
child abuse and neglect.

298. Research Relating to Children Bulletin. Washington, D. C.:
U. S. Children's Bureau, Clearinghouse for Research in
Child Life, 1949- . Irregular. HE19. 120.
Each issue of the Bulletin covers research in progress or
recently completed research in the area of child and family
life. The purpose, subject, method, findings, and any resulting publications are listed.

Standards

299. Areen, Judith. Standards Relating to Youth Service Agencies.
Cambridge, Mass.: Ballinger, 1977. 135p.
This publication is part of the Juvenile Justice Standards
Project of the IJA-ABA Joint Commission.

300. CWLA Standards for Adoption Service. Rev. ed. New York:
Child Welfare League of America, 1978. 101p.
More than just a set of standards, the CWLA series de-
fines the nature of the service, the place, its physical

setting, the role and responsibilities of each category of staff, and agency and administration planning. The CWLA periodically updates and revises the standards. The main section of the work is followed by a bibliography and an index. The CWLA Standards Services for Child Welfare include standards for foster family services, child protective services, homemaker services for children, services of child welfare institutions, day care services, services for unmarried parents, group-home services for children, and social work services for children in their own homes.

301. Standards for Day Care Centers for Infants and Children under Three Years of Age. Evanston, Ill. : American Academy of Pediatrics, Committee on the Infant and Pre-school Children, 1971. 23p.
This publication outlines the basic standards for quality day care as established by the American Academy of Pediatrics.

302. U. S. Children's Bureau. Standards for Specialized Courts Dealing with Children. Washington, D. C. : U. S. Government Printing Office, 1954. 99p. (Publication No. 346.)
In 1978 Greenwood Press reprinted the Bureau's standards on specialized courts for children. For more current standards see the American Bar Association's Juvenile Justice Standards Project Series published by Ballinger Press (items 299 and 324).

Survey

303. Child Protective Services Entering the 1980's: A Nationwide Survey. Englewood, Colo. : American Humane Associaton, 1981. 619p.
This nationwide survey describes the legal base, agency structure, and policy of each state's child protective services, along with specific data on program operations in over 1,200 county offices.

F. DAY CARE

Directory

304. Directory of Adult Day Care Centers. Baltimore, Md. : Health Standards/Quality Bureau, Department of Health and Human Services, 1980. 162p. S/N017-062-00124-3.
Issued on an irregular basis, the directory is a guide to approximately 700 programs that provide restorative, maintenance, or social programs for aged and handicapped in-

dividuals. Arranged geographically, entries give name, address, phone, name of director, date started, sponsor, funding source, type of program, and number of participants.

Guides

305. Boguslawski, Dorothy Beers. Guide for Establishing and Operating Day Care Centers for Young Children. New York: Child Welfare League of America, 1970. 100p. Written to supplement the Child Welfare League Association Standards for Day Care Service, this work is a practical guide on setting up and operating a day care center for preschool children. The appendixes contain suggested reading on day care, suppliers of day care equipment, and journals carrying articles on day care and the development of children.

306. Herbert-Jackson, Emily, and others. The Infant Center: A Complete Guide to Organizing and Managing Infant Day Care. Baltimore: University Park Press, 1977. 224p. The authors describe in detail ways to establish, organize, and operate an infant day care center. Parts 1 and 2 offer a general description of the day-to-day working of the center. Part 3 provides data on the quality control system that needs to operate to keep a system going and the final part offers help with the business and organizational aspects of an infant day care center. There are appendixes on readings, equipment, and supply lists.

307. Sciarra, Dorothy June. Developing and Administering a Child Day Care Center. Boston: Houghton Mifflin, 1979. 393p. Sciarra has written an introduction to the basic aspects of organizing and maintaining a day care center, including a large number of sample forms.

308. Zamoff, Richard. Guide to the Assessment of Day Care Services and Needs at the Community Level. Washington, D.C.: Urban Institute, 1971. This volume discusses procedures for the assessment of day care services at the community level and offers recommendations on research techniques for assessment of day care centers. The appendix contains research procedures, interview forms and related supplementary materials.

Standards

309. Child Welfare League of America Standards for Day Care Services. Rev. ed. New York: Child Welfare League of America, 1969. 123p.

Written for the social workers who need to know the principles of quality day care, these standards offer the essential details of organizing a day care center and the services, programs, and facilities it should provide.

310. Guidelines for Day Care Service. New York: Child Welfare League of America, 1972. 32p.
These guidelines are abstracted from the CWLA Standards for Day Care Services (item 309). A glossary and selected references conclude the work.

311. Standards for Day Care Centers for Infants and Children under Three Years of Age. Evanston, Ill.: American Academy of Pediatrics, Committee on the Infant and Preschool Children, 1971. 23p.
This publication outlines the basic standards for quality day care as established by the American Academy of Pediatrics.

G. DELINQUENCY AND CRIME

Abstracts

312. Crime and Delinquency Abstracts and Current Projects--An International Bibliography. Chevy Chase, Md.: National Institute of Mental Health, 1966- . Bimonthly, with annual cumulated index. FS2.22/13-4.
Each issue contains abstracts of current scientific and professional literature on crime and delinquency as well as accounts of ongoing research in crime and delinquency. Emphasis is on American material. The data base can be computer searched. Crime and Delinquency Abstracts continues the numbering and scope of International Bibliography on Crime and Delinquency.

313. Criminal Justice Abstracts. Paramus, N.J.: National Council on Crime and Delinquency, 1970- . Quarterly, with annual cumulative subject index.
Formerly Selected Highlights of Crime and Delinquency Literature, this service contains in-depth abstracts of current literature on crime and delinquency.

314. Criminology and Penology Abstracts. Amsteveleen, Netherlands: Kugler, 1961- . Bimonthly, with annual cumulation.
This abstracting service lists about 2,500 abstracts annually, most of them from U.S. and British journals. Articles abstracted cover crime and delinquency, control and treatment of offenders, criminal procedures, and administration of justice. Section 4.7 covers works on criminology and penology relevant to social work.

Bibliographies

315.   Boston, Guy, and others.   Criminal Justice and the Elderly:
           A Selected Bibliography.   Washington, D. C. :   National
           Council of Senior Citizens, 1979.   104p.
        The book's 150 entries are organized under four areas:
        Impact of Crime on Elderly, Elderly as Victims of Con-
        sumer Fraud, Victim Assistance and Restitution Pro-
        gram, and Involvement of Elderly in Criminal Justice
        System.

316.   Brantley, James R. , compiler.   Alternatives to Institutional-
           ization: A Definitive Bibliography.   Washington, D. C. :
           National Institute of Law Enforcement and Criminal
           Justice; distr.   Washington, D. C. :   U. S. Government
           Printing Office, 1979.   240p.   S/ N027-000-00820-8.
        This annotated bibliography lists 2,200 books; federal,
        state, and local documents; audiovisual materials; and
        doctoral dissertations on ways of avoiding institutionization,
        including halfway houses, work release, restitution, week-
        end sentencing, group and foster homes, probation, and
        parole.   All entries are taken from the National Criminal
        Justice Reference Service (NCJRS) data base.

317.   Crime and Juvenile Delinquency: A Bibliographic Guide to the
           Basic Microform Collection.   New Rochelle, N. Y. :
           Microfilm Corporation, 1977.   416p.
        The Microfilm Corporation has compiled a list of materials
        on crime and juvenile delinquency that are available on
        microfilm or microfiche.

318.   McCormick, Mona.   Probation, What the Literature Reveals:
           A Literature Review and Annotated Bibliography.   La
           Jolla, Calif. :   Western Behaviorial Institute, 1973.
           57p.
        McCormick has compiled a selective bibliography on pro-
        bation and written a brief introduction summarizing the
        literature.   Entries are mainly for the literature published
        in the 1960s and early 1970s.

Dictionary

319.   William, Virgil L.   Dictionary of American Penology: An
           Introductory Guide.   Westport, Conn. :   Greenwood,
           1979.   530p.
        The encyclopedia dictionary covers rehabilitation, com-
        munity based corrections, work release programs, homo-
        sexuality, political prisoners, recidivism, and many other
        topics.   Appendixes give U. S. Government statistics on
        crime and criminals, and addresses of organizations, agen-
        cies, and prison systems.

Directories

320. Directory of Legal Aid and Defender Offices in the United
States. Washington, D.C.: National Legal Aid and Defender Association, 1980. 149p.
Over 3,000 legal aid and defender organizations are cited
in this annual directory. Information on each organization
includes address, phone, and director's name.

321. Directory of Residential Treatment Centers. Cincinnati: International Halfway House Association, 1968- . Annual.
This publication lists public and private agencies affiliated
with the International Halfway House Association. The
agencies offer services to offenders, alcoholics, drug a-
busers, youth, and the mentally ill/retarded. Entries include name of program, address, phone, year established,
director's name, capacity, age and sex restrictions, and
primary function.

322. Juvenile and Adult Correctional Departments, Institutions,
Agencies, and Paroling Authorities in the United States
and Canada. College Park, Md.: American Correctional Association, 1955- . Annual.
The directory lists adult institutions, juvenile institutions,
juvenile and adult parole officers, and adult and juvenile
probation services. For each correctional facility, information is provided on name of institution, address, war-
den, capacity, population, and type of offense treated.

323. Nitzberg, Rita. Directory of Local Crime Prevention and
Victim Assistance. Washington, D.C.: Criminal Justice and the Elderly, 1980. 127p.
Sponsored by the National Council of Senior Citizens, the
directory describes more than 2,000 projects that offer
crime prevention, victim assistance, and crisis intervention services to the elderly and to the general public.
An appendix contains project-verified worksheets describing 500 programs.

Handbooks

324. Flicker, Barbara. Standards for Juvenile Justice: A Summary and Analysis. Cambridge, Mass.: Ballinger,
1977. 276p.
This publication analyzes the Institute of Judical Adminis-
tration/American Bar Association Juvenile Justice Standards Project. There are 10 volumes in the series relating to rights of minors, juvenile probation function,
transfer between courts, youth service agencies, planning
for juvenile justice, noncriminal behavior, monitoring,
sanctions, juvenile records and information systems, dispositional procedures, and counsel for private parties.

325. Glaser, Daniel, editor. Handbook of Criminology. Chicago: Rand McNally, 1974. 1,180p.
This handbook deals with all aspects of criminology and juvenile delinquency. There are three indexes: name, subject, and legal case.

326. Levin, Mark M., and Rosemary C. Sarri. Juvenile Delinquency: A Study of Juvenile Codes in the U.S. Ann Arbor: National Assessment of Juvenile Corrections, University of Michigan, 1974. 75p.
Prepared by a lawyer and a sociologist, this book analyzes and evaluates statutes that govern the processing of juveniles in juvenile courts in the 50 states and the District of Columbia.

Standards

327. Areen, Judith. Standards Relating to Youth Service Agencies. Cambridge, Mass.: Ballinger, 1977. 135p.
This publication is part of the Juvenile Justice Standards Project of the IJA-ABA Joint Commission.

328. U.S. Children's Bureau. Standards for Specialized Courts Dealing with Children. Washington, D.C.: U.S. Government Printing Office, 1954. 90p. (SRS)76-23041.
In 1978 Greenwood Press reprinted the Bureau's Standards on Specialized Courts for Children. For more current standards see the American Bar Association's Juvenile Justice Standards Project series published by Ballinger Press (items 324, 327, 612).

Statistics

329. Sourcebook of Criminal Justice Statistics. Washington, D.C.: National Criminal Justice Information and Statistics Service; distr. Washington, D.C.: U.S. Government Printing Office, 1973- . Irregular.
The work is a compilation of the latest criminal justice statistics. Arrangement is in four sections: Criminal Justice System Characteristics, Public Attitude Toward Crime, Nature of Known Offenses, Persons Arrested, and Judicial Processing and Correctional Supervision. All sources and references used in compiling the book are annotated.

H. ETHNIC GROUPS

Abstracts and Indexes

330. Asian American Reference Data Directory. Washington, D.C.:

U. S. Office for Asian American Affairs; distr. Washington, D. C. ; U. S. Government Printing Office, 1976. 481p. HE1. 2:As4.

Prepared by the Raj Associates for the Office for Asian American Affairs, this reference work has abstracts for some 480 books, articles, reports, government publications, data files, and reports relating to the health, education, and social welfare characteristics of Asian Americans. There are subgroup, subject, and geographic indexes.

331. Black Information Index. Herndon, Va. : Infonectics, 1970- . Bimonthly.

This is a bimonthly subject index to current sources of information on blacks. Over 80 periodicals, newspapers, and monographs are scanned. It covers all aspects of black life.

Bibliographies and Bibliographic Guides

332. Bell, Duran, and others. Delivering Services to Elderly Members of Minority Groups: A Critical Review of the Literature. Santa Monica, Calif. : Rand Corporation, 1976. 103p.

Sponsored by the U. S. Administration on Aging, the book is divided into two sections: a critical review of the literature on problems of elderly members of minority groups, followed by an extensive bibliography. The authors discuss the inadequacies of the social service delivery system to the Asian-American, Mexican-American, American Indian, and black elderly.

333. Bibliography on Racism, 1972-1975. Rockville, Md. ; National Institute of Mental Health, 1978. S/N017-024-00782-0.

Prepared by the Center for Minority Group Mental Health Programs, this bibliography continues the Center's Bibliography on Racism (1972).

334. Boyce, Byrl N. , and Sidney Turoff. Minority Groups and Housing: A Bibliography, 1950-1970. Morristown, N. J. : General Learning, 1972. 202p.

The authors have compiled a comprehensive, classified bibliography of books, pamphlets, articles, government publications and films on problems relating to housing for minority groups.

335. Brennan, Jere L. The Forgotten American--American Indians Remembered: A Selected Bibliography for Use in Social Work Education. New York: Council on Social Work Education, 1972. 82p.

Intended for use in social work education and social work practice, this bibliography is a partially annotated list of books, articles, and reference sources on the American Indian. Separate sections list American Indian newspapers and the area offices of the Bureau of Indian Affairs.

336. Buttlar, Lois, and Lubomyr Wynar. Building Ethnic Collections: An Annotated Guide for School Media Centers and Public Libraries. Littleton, Colo.: Libraries Unlimited, 1977. 434p.
An aid for building ethnic collections, print and nonprint, this guide provides listings for 2,300 items, arranged in 42 sections.

337. Cabello-Argandona, Roberto, and others. The Chicana: A Comprehensive Bibliographic Study. Los Angeles: University of California, Aztlan Publications, 1976. 200p.
This volume is a bibliography of 491 articles and books covering general reading, the Chicana and women's liberation movement, civil rights, culture and cultural processes, folk culture, economics, family, marriage, sex roles, history, education, politics, religion, labor, health, and nutrition. Most of the entries are annotated.

338. Dancy, Joseph. The Black Elderly: A Guide for Practitioners with Comprehensive Bibliography. Ann Arbor, Mich.: Institute of Gerontology, 1977. 56p.
Dancy identifies and describes a wide range of resources pertaining to the black elderly in America.

339. Davis, Lenwood G. The Black Aged in the United States: An Annotated Bibliography. Westport, Conn.: Greenwood, 1980. 216p.
This is a comprehensive listing of books, dissertations, theses, government publications, and articles on the black aged in the United States.

340. Davis, Lenwood G. The Black Family in the United States: A Selected Bibliography of Annotated Books, Articles, and Dissertations on Black Families in America. Westport, Conn.: Greenwood, 1978. 132p.
This annotated bibliography, containing citiations to 386 books, articles, and dissertations, provides a guide to social workers who wish to know more about the black family.

341. Davis, Lenwood G. The Black Woman in American Society: A Selected Annotated Bibliography. Boston: Hall, 1975. 159p.
This bibliography contains 1,186 citations covering works about black women from all periods of American history up to the 1970s. Works in the bibliography deal with the black family, culture, marriage, sex roles, education, health, and nutrition. About one third of the publication contains directory and statistical data: a directory of na-

tional organizations of black women, statistics on black
women in rural areas, listings of libraries with black history collections, and a list of black women elected officials.

342. Dunmore, Charlotte J. Black Children and Their Families:
     A Bibliography. San Francisco: R & E Research,
     1976. 103p.
     Dunmore has compiled 1,200 citations under eight head-
     ings: Adoption; Education; Health; Family Life; Life in
     the Ghetto; Mental Health; Sex, Contraception, and Family
     Planning; and Miscellaneous. Most of works were pub-
     lished between 1960 and 1975.

343. Dunmore, Charlotte J. Poverty, Participation, Protest,
     Power and Black Americans: A Selected Bibliography
     for Use in Social Work Education. New York: Council
     on Social Work Education, 1970. 67p.
     This is a selected bibliography of books, articles, and
     government publications on problems relating to black Amer-
     icans. There are sections on education, housing, econom-
     ics, mental health, family life, and social work.

344. Kitano, Harry H. L., compiler. Asians in America: A Se-
     lected Bibliography for Use in Social Work Education.
     New York: Council on Social Work Education, 1971.
     79p.
     This is an annotated bibliography of books and periodical
     articles on American-born Chinese, Japanese, Koreans,
     and Filipinos. Psychological and sociological problems,
     race and ethnic relations, economics, and immigration
     are the major areas explored. For a more detailed bib-
     liography of materials on Asians in America, see Isao
     Fujimoto's Asians in America: A Selected Annotated Bib-
     liography (1970).

345. Miller, Wayne Charles, editor. A Comprehensive Bibliography
     for the Studies of American Minorities. New York:
     New York University Press, 1976. 2 vols.
     This bibliography covers the history, religion, literature,
     sociology, and economics of American minorities. Chap-
     ters are arranged by ethnic group, and a short bibliogra-
     phic essay precedes each minority group bibliography.
     There are two indexes: author and title.

346. Navarro, Ekiseo. The Chicano Community: A Selected Bib-
     liography for Use in Social Work Education. New York:
     Council of Social Work Education, 1971. 57p.
     This annotated bibliography deals with Mexican-American
     acculturation, education, health, religion, family life, and
     social life. Each entry is given a code letter indicating
     the subject matter of the material, and a list of eight
     Chicano periodicals is appended. For another bibliography
     that identifies literature on Mexican-Americans see Jane

Talbot's A Comprehensive Chicano Bibliography, 1960-
1972 (Jenkins, 1973).

347. Obudho, Constance E. Black-White Racial Attitudes: An Annotated Bibliography. Westport, Conn.: Greenwood,
1976. 180p.
This bibliography has over 475 entries on black-white relations in the United States between 1950 and 1974. Subject areas are: Racial Attitude Formation and Change in
Children, Racial Attitudes in Young People, Racial Attitude
Change in Adults, Concomitants of Racial Attitudes, and
Racial Attitudes of Adults.

348. Padilla, Amado M., and Paul Arnada. Latino Mental Health:
Bibliography and Abstracts. Rockville, Md.: National
Institute of Mental Health, 1974. 288p. S/N1724-
00316.
There are over 490 abstracts on the psychological and
mental health of the Spanish surnamed, Spanish speaking,
or people of Spanish origin in the United States. The subject index completes the work. This publication supplements Latino Mental Health: A Review of the Literature,
(Rockville, Md.: National Institute of Mental Health,
1973).

349. Porter, Dorothy, compiler. The Negro in the United States:
A Selective Bibliography. Washington, D.C.: Library
of Congress, 1970. 313p. S/N030-000-00044-7.
This bibliography is a selected list of 1,781 items on the
black held by the Library of Congress. Arrangement is
by topic.

350. The Puerto Rican People: A Selected Bibliography for Use
in Social Work Education. New York: Council on Social Work Education, 1973. 54p.
Compiled by the Institute of Puerto Rican Studies at Brook-
lyn College, this annotated bibliography is intended for use
by social workers. The book is arranged by issues facing
the Puerto Rican community: Power, Politics and Government; Economics and Development; Social Welfare and Social Work; and Family Migration.

351. Reducing Racism in Mental Health Institutes and Delivery Systems: A Selected Bibliography. Washington, D.C.:
National Association of Social Workers, 1975. 3p.
This is a bibliography on reducing racism in social service agencies.

352. Reed, Katherine. Mental Health and Social Services for Mexican-Americans: An Essay and Annotated Bibliography.
Monticello, Ill.: Council of Planning Librarians, 1976.
37p.
This CPL bibliography examines books, articles, and re-

ports related to mental health and Mexican-Americans. A short essay introduces the bibliography.

353. Schlachter, Gail A., and Donna Belli. Minorities and Women: A Guide to Reference Literature in the Social Sciences. Los Angeles: Reference Service, 1977. 348p.
This reference work on the social, psychological, and political aspects of minorities and women annotates over 700 encyclopedias, dictionaries, almanacs, directories, indexes, abstracts, bibliographies, and biographies. There are three sets of indexes: author, title, and subject. Schlachter also has compiled A Guide to the Reference Literature on Women in the Social Sciences, Humanities, and Sciences (1981).

354. Sharma, Prakash C. A Selected Research Bibliography on Aspects of Socioeconomic and Political Life of Mexican Americans. Monticello, Ill.: Council of Planning Librarians, 1974. 19p.
This is a selected bibliography of books and articles on Mexican-Americans.

355. Woods, Richard. Reference Material on Mexican Americans: An Annotated Bibliography. Metuchen, N.J.: Scarecrow, 1976. 190p.
This bibliography lists 387 reference works on Mexican-Americans. Arrangement is by author.

Directories

356. American Indian Reference Book. Alexander, Va.: Earth, 1976. 308p.
This directory includes location of tribes and reservations, population figures, Indian schools, organizations, and selected books and nonbook materials.

357. Bundy, Mary Lee, and Irvin Gilchrist, editors. The National Civil Rights Directory and Organizations Directory. College Park, Md.: Urban Information Interpreters, 1979. 183p.
This directory lists civil rights organizations. For each group information includes name, address, phone, objectives, activities, and organizational structure. An appendix concludes the work.

358. Cole, Katherine W. Minority Organizations: A National Directory. Garrett Park, Md.: Garrett Park, 1978. 385p.
This directory contains 3,250 organizations established by minority groups or for the benefit of minority groups. Information for each organization includes name, address, phone, and purpose. Included are an alphabetical index to the

name of the organization, a geographical index, a functional index, and a glossary.

359. Johnson, Willis L. Directory of Special Programs for Minority Group Members: Career Information Services, Employment Skills Banks, Financial Aid Sources. 3rd ed. Garrett Park, Md.: Garrett Park, 1980. 612p.
This directory lists career and job information, employment information, and scholarship information for minorities.

360. National Directory of Hispanic Professionals and Human Services in Mental Health Organizations. Washington, D.C.: National Coalition of Hispanic Mental Health and Human Services, 1977/78- . Biennial.
This directory lists 75 mental health community programs and 1,250 Hispanic social service professionals.

361. Wasserman, Paul. Ethnic Information Sources of the United States: A Guide to Organizations, Agencies, Foundations, Institutions, Media, Commercial and Trade Bodies, Government Programs.... Detroit: Gale, 1976. 751p.
The subtitle is "A Guide to Organizations, Agencies, Foundations, Institutions, Media, Commercial and Trade Bodies, Government Programs, Research Institutions, Libraries and Museums, Religious Organizations, Banking Firms, Festivals and Fairs, Travel and Tourist Offices, Airlines and Ship Lines, Book Dealers and Publishers, Representatives, and Books, Pamphlets and Audio-visuals on Specific Ethnic Groups." The book includes charitable organizations, foundations, and social service agencies.

362. Wynar, Lubomyr R. Encyclopedic Directory of Ethnic Organizations in the United States. Littleton, Colo.: Libraries Unlimited. 1975. 440p.
This directory identifies and describes 1,500 social, welfare, religious, fraternal, professional, scholarly, and political agencies representing 73 ethnic groups. Information on each organization includes address, phone, offices, publications, meetings, membership, and goals. A separate section provides a selective listing of major multiethnic and research-oriented nonethnic groups involved in the study of ethnic organizations.

Encyclopedia

363. Reference Encyclopedia of the American Indian. 3rd ed. Rye, N.Y.: Todd, 1978. 2 vols.
Volume 1 contains listings and information on government agencies at all levels, museums, libraries, urban Indian centers, reservations, tribal councils, schools, publications,

and instructional aids. Also part of Volume 1 is a classified and annotated bibliography of over 2,500 books. Volume 2 has short biographical sketches of prominent living American Indians and non-Indians active in Indian affairs. The first edition of this encyclopedia was published in one volume in 1967.

Handbooks

364. Gill, George A. A Reference Resource Guide to the American Indian. Tempe: Center for Indian Education, Arizona State University, 1974. 187p.
Information is provided on all aspects of American Indians. Separate chapters list government agencies, tribal councils and Indian organizations, religious groups, libraries, book publishers, audiovisual materials, Indian self-help programs, and Indian education programs.

365. U. S. Commission on Civil Rights. Puerto Ricans in the Continental United States: An Uncertain Future. Washington, D. C. : U. S. Government Printing Office, 1976. 157p. CR1. 2:P96r/2.
Essays dealing with jobs, income, and demography, plus statistical data and recommendations for improving the condition of Puerto Ricans are included. A selected bibliography completes the report. The U. S. Commission on Civil Rights has also prepared a report on The Navajo Nation: An American Colony (1975) and The American Indian Civil Rights Handbook (1972).

Almanac

366. Ploski, Harry A. , and Warren Mark III, compilers. Negro Almanac: A Reference Work on the Afro-American. Bicentennial ed. New York: Bellwether, 1976. 1,206p. This reference work consists of a chronology of black history since 1600, a section on black social and cultural life, biographical sketches, a bibliography, and selected statistics.

I. FAMILY

Bibliographies and Bibliographical Guides

367. Aldous, Joan, editor. Inventory of Marriage and Family Literature, Vol. 3, 1973/74- . St. Paul: Family Social Science, University of Minnesota, 1975- .
The inventory continues the International Bibliography of Research in Marriage and the Family.

This bibliography surveys the international research on marriage and the family covering the period between 1965 and 1972. There are four sections: KWIC index, a subject index, an author listing, and a listing of periodicals. Textbooks and unpublished materials have been excluded, but some non-English language sources are included.

368. Aldous, Joan, and Nancy Dahl, editors. International Bibliography of Research in Marriage and the Family, Vols. 1-2, 1965-1972. Minneapolis: University of Minnesota Press for the Minnesota Family Study Center and the Institute of Life Insurance, 1974. 2 vols.

369. Annotated Bibliography on Unmarried Fathers. New York: National Council on Illegitimacy, 1969. 13p.
This bibliography deals with the literature on unmarried fathers.

370. Blank, Marion S., compiler. Working with People: A Selected Social Casework Bibliography. New York: Family Service Association of America, 1978. 94p.
This classified bibliography, compiled by the Boston University School of Social Work, was designed for use in the social work classroom. The book is structured in six major parts: Basic Readings, Essential Elements of Practice, Special Problems, Evaluation, Additional Frames of Reference and Some New Approaches to Casework, and Issues in Casework Practice. The entries are not annotated.

371. Brown, Daniel G. Behavior Modification in Child, School and Family Mental Health: An Annotated Bibliography on Applications with Parents and Teachers and in Marriage and Family Counseling. Champaign, Ill.: Research Press, 1972. 105p.
This publication contains abstracts of books and articles on behavior therapy and the care and treatment of mentally handicapped children.

372. Family Life and Child Development, 1972: A Selective Annotated Bibliography. New York: Child Study, 1973. 52p.
Compiled by the Child Study Association of America, this annotated bibliography contains books and pamphlets published between 1962 and 1972. The entries have been classified under three headings: Marriage and the Family, Child Development, and Sex Education. There is an author-title index.

373. Family Life and Child Development: A Selective, Annotated Bibliography, 1973. New York: Child Study, 1974. 48p.
This book contains a list of 284 books and pamphlets, published between 1963 and 1973, about social issues that af-

fect family life and the community. Publications are ar-
ranged in sections on Marriage and the Family, Human
Development, Sex Education, Children with Disabilities,
Schools and Learning, Mental Health Education, and Social
Problems and the Family.

374. Glick, Ira D., and Jay Haley. Family Therapy and Research:
An Annotated Bibliography of Articles and Books Published 1950-1970. New York: Grune and Stratton,
1971. 280p.
Originally appearing in Changing Families, this bibliography
surveys the research literature in family therapy published
between 1950 and 1970. The entries are organized under
four headings: Family Descriptions, Types of Families,
Literature Surveys, and Books. Sociological and anthro-
pological works and popular books and articles have been
excluded from the bibliography. There is an author index.

375. Israel, Stanley, compiler and editor. A Bibliography on Divorce. New York: Block, 1974. 300p.
Over 150 books published in the United States from the
1940s to the 1970s are represented in this classified bibliography. All aspects of divorce--legal, sociological,
and religious--are explored.

376. McCormick, Mona. Stepfather, What the Literature Reveals:
A Literature Review and Annotated Bibliography. La
Jolla, Calif.: Western Behavioral Sciences Institute,
1974. 75p.
This bibliography consists of a concise overview of the
literature on the stepfather. About 100 items are annotated.

377. McKenney, Mary. Divorce: A Selected Annotated Bibliography.
Metuchen, N.J.: Scarecrow, 1975. 157p.
Topics covered are General and Historical Works, Legal
Aspects, Financial Aspects, Statistics, Divorce Outside
the U.S., Women Divorcees, Men Divorcees, Children of
Divorce, Psychological and Sociological Aspects, Religious
and Moral Aspects, and Miscellaneous Works. Appendixes
include resource people and American divorce laws by
state. Author and subject indexes are included.

378. Schlesinger, Benjamin. The Jewish Family: A Survey and
Annotated Bibliography. Toronto: University of Toronto
Press, 1971. 175p.
The volume annotates books on various aspects of Jewish
family life in Asia, Africa, Latin America, the U.S.,
and Canada. Statistical appendixes accompany the bibliography.

379. Schlesinger, Benjamin. The One Parent Family: Perspec-

tives and Annotated Bibliography. 3rd ed. Toronto:
University of Toronto Press, 1970. 138p.
Intended as an aid for social work students and practitioners, this annotated bibliography covers aspects of the one-
parent family--marriage, family desertion and separation,
divorce, widowhood, unmarried parents, and remarriage.
The first part consists of three essays on the one-parent
family, and the second part of the book is an annotated
list of 280 books, pamphlets, and journal articles published
through 1970. A statistical appendix is included as well
as other sources related to the field of the one-parent
family.

380. Selective Guide to Materials for Mental Health and Family
Life Education. New York: Mental Health Materials
Center, 1976. 947p.
This volume contains evaluations of books, pamphlets,
films, and audiovisuals on mental health. Subject areas
covered include alcoholism, drug abuse, suicide and crisis
intervention, developmental disabilities, mental illness,
etc. A final section is devoted to additional reference
sources.

381. Sell, Betty H., and Kenneth D. Sell. Divorce in the United
States, Canada, and Great Britain: A Guide to Information Sources. Detroit: Gale, 1978. 298p.
The Sells have compiled a comprehensive bibliography that
covers the entire spectrum of divorce in the U.S., Canada,
and Great Britain.

382. Trojan, Judith. American Family Life Films. Metuchen,
N.J.: Scarecrow, 1981. 425p.
The author, a film evaluator for the Educational Film Library Association, has prepared a comprehensive guide to
16mm films on family life in America. Information on
each film includes description of contents, length of film,
whether black-and-white or color, distributor, and director. Areas of interest to social service professionals are
separation and divorce, family counseling, single parenting
and stepparenting, fatherhood, and mental health.

383. U.S. Children's Bureau. Foster Family Services: Selected
Reading List. Washington, D.C.: U.S. Government
Printing Office, 1977. 78p. S/N017-090-00030-5.
This bibliography is a guide to selected books, pamphlets,
and articles on the topic of foster care.

384. U.S. Mental Health Materials Center. A Selective Guide to
Materials for Mental Health and Family Life Education.
Northfield, Ill.: Perennial Education, 1972. 841p.
This list reviews governmental and nongovernmental edu-
cational publications and films on mental health, family
life, alcoholism, drug abuse, and suicide prevention.

Dictionary

385.	Glass, Stuart M. A Divorce Dictionary: A Book for You
        and Your Children. Boston: Little, Brown, 1979. 71p.
        Prepared for grades 4 through 6, this small dictionary
        contains definitions ranging from a few sentences to several
        pages on the terminology of divorce. It is illustrated with
        line drawings.

Directories

386.	Princeton Center for Infancy and Early Childhood. Parents'
        Yellow Pages. Edited by Frank Caplan. Garden City,
        N. Y.: Anchor, 1978. 571p.
        This basic reference source for parents of infants has
        chapters on abortion, nutrition, health, education, etc.
        Each section has an annotated bibliography and list of ser-
        vice organizations.

387.	Directory of Foundations Supporting Child-and-Family-Serving
        Organizations. Washington, D. C.: Child Welfare League
        of America, Center for Governmental Affairs, 1978.
        The directory describes in detail 315 foundations that made
        grants in 1978 to organizations involved in services to
        children and/or families.

388.	Directory of Homemaker-Home Health Aide Services. New
        York: National HomeCaring Council, 1979. 325p.
        Over 145 local agencies supplying homemaker and health
        aide services that are accredited/approved by the Council
        are included in the directory.

389.	Directory of Homemaker-Home Health Aide Services in the
        United States, Puerto Rico and the Virgin Islands, 1980.
        New York: National HomeCaring Council, 1980. 375p.
        This directory lists over 5,000 accredited/approved home-
        maker and health aide programs in the U. S. The computer-
        assisted data base is updated quarterly.

390.	Family Service Association Directory of Member Agencies.
        New York: The Association, 1910- . Annual.
        This directory contains the official list of member agencies
        and provisional member agencies of the Family Service
        Association of America, with current addresses, executive
        directors, and areas served by each agency. Arrangement
        is in two sections: one on the United States (alphabetically
        by state) and one on Canada (alphabetically by province).

391.	Register of Health Service Providers in Marital/Family Ther-
        apy. Claremont, Calif.: American Association of Mar-
        riage and Family Counselors, 1980. 221p. Biennial.

This register contains an alphabetical and geographical list of 5,000 clinical members, affiliates, and honorary life members of the American Association of Marriage and Family Counselors.

392. Tansey, Anne M. Where to Get Help for Your Family. Rev. and enl. St. Meinrad, Ind.: Abbey, 1977. 204p.
Written for the nonprofessional, this book covers 157 social service agencies with a brief history of each agency. It also lists current activities, publications, areas of interest, special projects, and address. Types of agencies included range from the American Humane Association to National Urban League to American Institute of Family Relations to National Council of Senior Citizens to Big Brothers of America. Agencies are organized by general categories.

Factbook

393. Family Factbook. Chicago: Marquis, 1978. 676p.
This useful reference book provides essays and statistics on all aspects of the family. The volume has seven sections: Family (general), Adults, Children, Health, Work and Income, Housing, and Index.

Handbooks

394. Duncan, Cora, and others. A Guide for Board Members of Voluntary Family Service Agencies. New York: Family Service Association of America, 1975. 46p.
Intended for family service boards of directors, this manual discusses the specifics of creating and maintaining an effective volunteer board.

395. Kravse, Harry D. Family Law in a Nutshell. St. Paul, Minn.: West, 1977. 400p.
Kravse has written a concise summary of family law for social workers.

396. Stone, Helen D., and Jeanne M. Hunzeker. Creating a Foster Parent-Agency: A Handbook. New York: Child Welfare League of America, 1978. 44p.
Stone's pamphlet discusses foster home evaluation, keeping child's handbooks, foster parent-agency agreements, program guides for foster parent neighborhood groups, and service evaluations.

Standards

397. Proposed Provisions for the Accreditation of Agencies Serving

Families and Children: Draft 1. New York: Family
Service Association of America, 1977. 81p.
A special committee of the Family Service Association of
America prepared draft guidelines for accreditation of
agencies serving families and children.

398. Standards for Foster Family Service. New York: Child Welfare League of America, 1975. 125p.
A revision of the 1959 League's Standards for Foster Family Care Service, this volume outlines the nature of foster
family service and the roles and responsibilities of each
catagory of staff, agency, organization, and administration.

399. Standards for Services to Unmarried Parents. New York:
Child Welfare League of America, 1971. 89p.
These standards define the highest quality of practice in
service to unmarried parents.

Survey

400. Annual Price Survey: Family Budget Costs. New York:
Budget Standard Service, Community Council of Greater
New York, 1956- . Annual.
This annual price survey sponsored by the Community
Council of Greater New York estimates the budget costs
of maintaining a moderate level of living in New York
City. The survey documents the impact that inflation has
on various family types.

J. FAMILY PLANNING

Abstracts

401. Current Literature in Family Planning. New York: Planned
Parenthood Federation of America, 1972- . Monthly.
International in coverage, this annotated bibliography and
abstract is designed for social workers who wish to keep
up to date on family planning literature. Entries include
summaries or abstracts of articles from 175 professional
journals, pamphlets, and books.

Bibliographies

402. Abortion Bibliography. Troy, N. Y.: Whitston, 1970- .
Annual.
This bibliography contains books and articles on the subject of abortion and related topics. The entries are divided in two major groupings: a title section and a subject section. There is an author index.

403. Atkins, Jacqueline Marx, compiler. Audio-Visual Resources for Population Education and Family Planning: An International Guide for Social Work Education. New York: International Association of Schools of Social Work, 1975. 148p.
Prepared by the International Association of Schools of Social Work for use in classrooms, this guide provides information on audiovisual equipment, filmstrips, films, transparencies, slides with sources for purchase, and price. A bibliography of articles and books is included. Introductory essays give an overview of the materials and uses for these materials for population education and family planning.

404. Lyle, Katherine Ch'iu, and Sheldon Jerome Segal, editors. International Family Planning Programs, 1966-1975: A Bibliography. New York: Population Council, 1977. 207p.
Although international in scope, the bibliography does emphasize family planning in the U.S. It covers medical, sociological, and behavioral literature including books, chapters of books, conference reports, and journal articles mostly published in English from 1966 to 1975. Arrangement is by county with a section on the general aspects of family planning.

405. National Clearinghouse for Family Planning. Catalog of Family Planning Materials. Rockville, Md.: Bureau of Community Health Services, 1979. 144p. S/N017-026-00076-3.
This bibliography of books, articles, and audiovisual aids covers birth control, contraceptives, venereal diseases, abortion, etc.

406. Watts, Mary E., compiler. Selected References for Social Workers on Family Planning: An Annotated List. Rev. ed. Rockville, Md.: Maternal and Child Health Service, Department of Health, Education and Welfare, 1971. 38p. HL20-2759:501.
This volume contains an annotated list of books, articles, and pamphlets on the subject of family planning. Most of the entries appeared prior to 1970.

Directories

407. Directory--Family Planning Grantees and Clinics. 3rd ed. Rockville, Md.: National Clearinghouse for Family Planning, 1979. 105p. HE20.5102:062/3.
This publication lists 200 grantees and over 3,600 family planning clinics supported by the Bureau of Community Health Service. The entries are arranged geographically.

408. Directory--Family Planning Service Sites--United States.

Washington, D. C. : Center for Health Statistics, Department of Health, Education and Welfare, 1977. 181p. HE20. 6202:F21/2.
This directory summarizes the responses of 4,700 medical family planning agencies that responded from the 5,600 in the National Inventory of Family Planning Services.

K. HANDICAPPED

Abstracts

409. DSH Abstracts. Washington, D. C. : Deafness, Speech and Hearing Publications, 1960- . Quarterly.
International in scope, DSH cites abstracts on the most significant current literature on deafness and on speech and hearing disorders. This abstracting service covers articles and books from a wide variety of disciplines, including social work.

410. Developmental Disabilities Abstracts. Washington, D. C. : U. S. Division of Developmental Disabilities, 1977- .
Quarterly, annual cumulated index.
Originally entitled Mental Retardation Abstracts (1964-1973) and Mental Retardation and Developmental Disabilities Abstracts (1974-1976), this work abstracts nearly 3,600 scientific and professional articles per year from books and journals on mental retardation. It has author and subject indexes.

411. Rehabilitation Literature. Chicago: National Society for Crippled Children and Adults, 1940- . Bimonthly.
Issues contain abstracts of articles, books, and pamphlets concerned with care, education, and employment of the handicapped. Arrangement of the abstracts is by subject.
Author indexes in each issue are cumulated into an annual index in the January issue.

Bibliographies and Bibliographical Guides

412. Baskin, Barbara Holland. Notes from a Different Drummer: A Guide to Juvenile Fiction Portraying the Handicapped.
New York: Bowker, 1977. 375p.
The volume is arranged in five chapters: Society and the Handicapped; Literary Treatment of Disability; Assessing and Using Juvenile Fiction Portraying the Disabled; Patterns and Trends in Juvenile Fiction, 1940-1975; and An Annotated Guide to Juvenile Fiction Portraying the Handicapped (which forms the bulk of the work). The entries are organized into nine descriptive categories to indicate the type of impairment.

413. Bauman, Mary K. , compiler. Blindness, Visual Impairment, Deaf-Blindness: An Annotated Listing of the Literature, 1953-1975. Philadelphia: Temple University, 1977. 537p.
Directed toward individuals who work with the visually handicapped, this is a subject listing of books, pamphlets, and research material on the visually handicapped selected from the card catalog of the Reference Library and Research Center for Sensory Disabilities, Temple University. Medical literature has been excluded. There is an author index, an analytical subject index, and a list of associations and organizations in the U.S. , Canada, and the U.K.

414. Dumas, Neil S. , and John E. Muthard, editors. Rehabilitation Research and Demonstration Projects, 1955-1970. Gainesville: Regional Rehabilitation Research Institute, University of Florida, 1970. 412p.
This retrospective bibliography contains all the publications resulting from the research and demonstration projects supported by the U.S. Social and Rehabilitation Service.

415. Fellendorf, George W. , editor. Bibliography on Deafness: A Selected Index. Rev. ed. Washington, D.C. : Alexander Graham Bell Association for the Deaf, 1977. 272p.
The bibliography indexes articles printed in the Volta Review, 1899-1976 and American Annals of the Deaf, 1847-1976. The entries are found under 44 categories. The new edition lists entries by publication with the oldest entry appearing first.

416. Guide to Films About Blindness. New York: American Foundation for the Blind, 1978. 93p.
The guide contains over 175 films, videocassettes, and slide shows dealing with blindness and services to blind persons.

417. Hale, Glorya, editor. The Source Book for the Disabled: An Illustrated Guide to Easier and More Independent Living for Physically Disabled People, Their Families and Friends. New York: Paddington, 1979. 288p.
The stated purpose of this publication is to provide "a more independent living for the disabled." The last section lists leaflets, books, and periodicals for further reading and gives the addresses of organizations and government agencies, special interest groups, and commercial sources of aids and equipment in both Britain and the U.S. Illustrations of various types of aids form a very important part of the book.

418. Library Aids and Services Available to the Blind and Visually Handicapped. Columbus, Ohio: Delta Gamma Executive Offices, 1972. 40p.

This directory is a guide to materials of special interest to the blind and visually handicapped and those who work with the visually handicapped. Included is information on sources for obtaining talking books, books in Braille, records, and tapes.

419. McCormick, Mona. Primary Education for the Disadvantaged, What the Literature Reveals: A Literature Review and Annotated Bibliography. La Jolla, Calif.: Western Behavioral Sciences Institute, 1975. 105p.
Compiled as a background literature search for a Western Behavioral Sciences Institute study, the volume consists of an overview of primary education for the disadvantaged with a lengthy annotated bibliography.

420. May, Marianne, editor. Low Vision Literature Pertaining to Education and Rehabilitation: A Keyword Index. New York: American Foundation for the Blind, 1978. 355p.
May has prepared a keyword index to more than 900 books, articles, monographs, and dissertations that deal with education and rehabilitation of individuals with low vision.

421. Scholl, Geraldine, and Ronald Schnur. Measures of Psychological, Vocational, Educational Functioning in the Blind and Visually Handicapped. New York: American Foundation for the Blind, 1976. 94p.
The authors have compiled an annotated bibliography and index to measures of personality, and occupational, psychological, and educational functioning in the blind and visually handicapped.

422. Selected Publications Concerning the Handicapped. Washington, D.C.: U.S. Office for the Handicapped, 1974. 45p. HE1.18:H19.
This bibliography contains selected publications on the rehabilitation of the handicapped.

423. Weiss, Louise. Access to the World: A Travel Guide for the Handicapped. New York: Chatham Square, 1977. 178p.
This publication provides an annotated list of guidebooks for the handicapped. Arranged country by country, state by state, the entries cover automobiles, recreational vehicles, buses, trains, airplanes, and travel agencies throughout the world. The U.S. Office of Public Affairs, Federal Aviation Administration has prepared Access Travel: Airports (1979), which describes 220 airports in 27 countries, with facilities and services of special importance to persons in wheelchairs and the blind, deaf, and aged.

424. Wright, Keith C. Library and Information Services for Handicapped Individuals. Littleton, Colo.: Libraries Unlimited, 1979. 196p.

The author, Dean of the College of Library and Information
Services at the University of Maryland, provides an overview to the literature on blind and visually impaired; mentally handicapped; and aging and physically handicapped
persons. Appended are a glossary of acronyms, a list
of selected organizations providing services to handicapped
individuals, and a directory of selected sources for the
handicapped.

Dictionary

425. Boatner, Maxine T., and John E. Gates. Dictionary of Idioms
for the Deaf. Rev. ed. Woodbury, N. Y.: Barron,
1975. 392p.
This dictionary defines over 4,000 words and phrases most
likely to be difficult for the deaf to understand.

Directories

426. American Annals of the Deaf--Reference Issue. Silver Spring,
Md.: American Annals of the Deaf, 1847- . Annual.
The annual reference issue of AAD describes various educational facilities for the deaf and hard-of-hearing. Included are the names of religious personnel for the deaf
in the U.S., camps for the deaf, organizations for the
deaf in the U.S., homes for aged deaf, speech and hearing centers, and American instructors for the deaf.

427. Bruck, Lilly. Access: The Guide to a Better Life for Disabled Americans. New York: Ohst, 1978. 251p.
Designed for the handicapped and those helping the handicapped, this consumer guide provides information on services, government agencies, and publications pertaining
to the disabled.

428. Directory of Agencies Serving the Visually Handicapped in the
United States. New York: American Foundation for the
Blind, 1969/70- . Biennial.
This directory, formerly Directory of Agencies Serving
Blind Persons in the United States, provides information
on state, local, and special agencies serving the blind and
visually handicapped. Each entry includes the name of
the agency, address and telephone number, director, date
established, services provided, and associations of membership. The first edition of the directory was published
in 1926.

429. Directory of Educational Facilities for Learning Disabled.
Novato, Calif.: Academic Therapy, 1973- .
Biennial.
The directory contains an alphabetical listing by state of

over 400 private and remedial schools and diagnostic centers providing services to the learning disabled in the
United States. Information on each agency includes address, telephone number, name of director, as well as
other useful data.

430. Directory of Information Resources for the Handicapped. Santa
Monica, Calif. : Ready Reference, 1980. 236p.
This directory is organized into six chapters: Advocacy,
Consumer, and Voluntary Health Organizations; Information
Data Banks; Federal Government Other Than Information;
Professional and Trade Organizations; Facilities, Schools,
and Clinics; and Service Organizations. Information for
each entry includes address, phone, handicapping condition
served or studied, history of organization, and type of in-
formation provided.

431. Directory of National Information Sources on Handicapping Conditions and Related Services. 2nd ed. Washington,
D. C. : U. S. Office for Handicapping Conditions and Related Services, 1980. 236p. S/ N017-091-00234-7.
This directory lists over 270 national organizations (private and public) that help the handicapped with direct services or information. Organizations are grouped into various categories. For each organization the directory gives
the name, address, handicapping condition served, and
types of services available. The index is arranged by
handicap and by subject.

432. Directory of Organizations Interested in the Handicapped. 1976
ed. Washington, D. C. : Committee for the Handicapped,
People to People Program, 1975. 48p.
Published every three years, this annotated directory provides information on organizations that assist the handicapped. Many of the groups included are specialized, such
as the Academy of Dentistry for the Handicapped and the
World Rehabilitation Fund, Inc.

433. Federal Assistance for Programs Serving the Handicapped.
Washington, D. C. : U. S. Office of Handicapped Individuals, 1977. 333p. HE1. 2:A57/ 3.
This book provides a description of over 200 federal assistance programs for the handicapped. Each entry gives
a description of use and user restrictions, types of assistance, eligibility requirements, application procedure, appropriations, program accomplishments, enabling legislation, and information contacts. The majority of programs
in this directory are not in the Catalog of Federal Domestic Assistance (item 33). The U. S. Office of Handicapped
Individuals, Department of Health and Human Services, updates the directory periodically.

434. Federal Assistance for Programs Serving the Visually

Handicapped. 5th ed. New York: American Foundation for the Blind, 1979. 61p.
Based on the Catalog of Federal Domestic Assistance (item 33), the 5th edition has information on 19 federal agencies offering 139 programs for the blind or funding other programs for the blind. Entries include agency name, address, program name, and description. Programs are listed according to federal agency. The directory is updated annually.

435. Gollay, Elinor, and Alwina Bennett. The College Guide for Students with Disabilities: A Detailed Directory of Higher Education Services, Programs, and Facilities Accessible to Handicapped Students in the United States. Cambridge, Mass.: Abt; Boulder, Colo.: Westview, 1976. 545p.
Although not comprehensive in its coverage, this directory does list college and university programs that have been designed to meet the needs of handicapped students.

436. International Guide to Aids and Appliances for Blind and Visually Impaired Persons. New York: American Foundation for the Blind, 1977. 255p.
The directory provides detailed information on over 270 sources worldwide for 2,500 special devices for blind and visually handicapped persons.

437. Zang, Barbara, editor. How to Get Help for Kids: A Reference Guide to Services for Handicapped Children. Syracuse, N.Y.: Gaylord, 1980. 245p.
The author, network organizer for the Children's Defense Fund, lists 2,000 agencies working with handicapped children. Six essays, an annotated bibliography, sources of recreational services, and an organization index round out the work.

Guidelines

438. Spungin, Susan Jay, editor. Guidelines for Public School Programs Serving the Visually Handicapped. New York: American Foundation for the Blind, 1978. 60p.
Of interest to school social workers, this volume outlines administrative guidelines for state and local educational agencies concerned with the educational placement of the handicapped under Public Law 94-142, the Education for All Handicapped Children Act. The appendix includes further readings and a list of state, local, and regional organizations able to perform various services to handicapped individuals.

Handbooks

439. Burgdorf, Robert L., Jr., editor. The Legal Rights of Handicapped Persons: Cases, Materials and Text. Baltimore: Brookes, 1980. 1,127p.
Designed for use in law school courses, the book covers all legal areas where the handicapped have been denied rights or benefits. Chapters include employment, access to buildings, transportation systems, freedom from residential confinement, equal access to medical services, procreation, marriage, and raising children.

440. Handbook for Blind College Students. Des Moines, Iowa: National Federation of the Blind, 1975. 36p.
A guide to libraries, rehabilitation, and other services available to blind college students.

441. Kauffman, James, and Daniel Hallahan, editors. Handbook of Special Education. Englewood Cliffs, N.J.: Prentice-Hall, 1981. 807p.
This reference book provides thorough coverage of special education.

442. 94-142 and 504: Numbers That Add Up to Educational Rights for Handicapped Children. Washington, D.C.: Children's Defense Fund, 1978. 52p.
This handbook details HHR regulations in Public Law 94-142 and Section 504 of the Rehabilitation Act of 1973 and ways social workers can use these to secure rights for handicapped children.

443. Roberts, Joseph, and Bonnie Hawk. Legal Rights Primer for the Handicapped In and Out of the Classroom. Novato, Calif.: Academic Therapy, 1980. 160p.
This book outlines the rights of handicapped in and out of the classroom. The book includes a summary of Section 504 and the complete text of PL94-142.

444. Weisse, Fran Alexander, and Mimi Winer. Coping with Sight Loss: The Vision Resource Book. Newton, Mass.: Vision Foundation, 1981. 219p.
An updated version of Winer's Information and Resources for the Newly Blind and Visually Handicapped of Massachusetts (1977), this book explains the legal definition of blindness, how to locate an eye doctor, and so on. It covers national agencies and organizations, financial benefits, legal rights, careers, sports, and transportation for the handicapped. The last part of the book contains information on state resources for Massachusetts residents.

L. HEALTH CARE

Abstracts and Indexes

445. Abstracts of Health Care Management Studies. Ann Arbor,
        Mich.: Health Administration Press, 1978- .
        Quarterly, with annual cumulation.
        Superseding Abstracts of Hospital Management Studies, this
        international journal abstracts studies of management, plan-
        ning, and public policy related to the delivery of health
        care. Sources abstracted include journals, books, govern-
        ment publications, dissertations, reports, and other un-
        published research. Entries are classified and include
        health services and social services.

446. Biological Abstracts. Philadelphia: Biosciences Information
        Service, 1926- . Semimonthly.
        This abstract covers the world's bioscience research re-
        ports. Abstracts are arranged by broad subject areas,
        with subheadings and numerous cross-references. Areas
        of interest to social workers include gerontology, pedia-
        trics, psychiatry, public health, and social biology.

447. Cumulative Index to Nursing and Allied Health Literature.
        Glendale, Calif.: Seventh Day Adventist Hospital As-
        sociation, 1961- . Bimonthly, with annual cumula-
        tion.
        CINAHL indexes all major English language nursing jour-
        nals plus popular magazines and biomedical and social
        service journals. Appendixes serve as guides to audio-
        visual materials, book reviews, pamphlets, files, film-
        strips, and records. This series continues the Cumulative
        Index to Nursing Literature.

448. Hospital Literature Index. Chicago: American Hospital As-
        sociation, 1957- . Quarterly, with annual cumula-
        tion.
        HLI is a subject and author index to English language ar-
        ticles on all aspects of the delivery of health care with
        emphasis on management, planning, and financing. Each
        issue includes a list of recent acquisitions in the library
        of the Association.

449. Index Medicus. Bethesda, Md.: National Library of Medicine,
        1960- . Monthly. Cumulated annually as Cumulated
        Index Medicus.
        Index Medicus provides author and subject access to articles
        in all fields of medicine, including medical social work,
        psychiatric social work, public health, and health care.
        MEDLARS (the Medical Literature Analysis and Retrieval
        System of the National Library of Medicine) data base can
        be searched by computer.

Bibliographies and Bibliographical Guides

450. Chen, Ching-chih. Health Sciences Information Sources. Cambridge, Mass.: M.I.T. Press, 1981. 766p.
This bibliography annotates over 4,000 books on all aspects of the health sciences.

451. Lunin, Lois F. Health Sciences and Services: A Guide to the Literature. Detroit: Gale, 1979. 614p.
This volume is an annotated inventory of information sources including publications, data bases, and organizations of the disciplines that comprise the health sciences. Of interest to social workers are the sections on hospitals and nursing homes, health insurance, public health, and general health sciences and services.

452. Morris, Dwight A. Health Care Administration: A Guide to Information Sources. Detroit: Gale, 1978. 264p.
This volume is confined to materials on health facility management, including hospitals and long-term care, mental health, and ambulatory care facilities. All entries are evaluated and annotated. The appendixes list libraries and information centers, associations, individual sources, publishers, and graduate schools in health care administration. There are author/title and subject indexes.

453. Pinel, Patricia N. Comprehensive Bibliography on Health Maintenance Organizations: 1970-1973. Denver, Colo.: Medical Group Management Association, 1974. 96p.
Pinel has prepared an in-depth bibliography on ancillary health service organizations.

454. Rees, Alan, and Blanche A. Young. The Consumer Health Information Source Book. New York: Bowker, 1981. 450p.
Prepared for both the consumer and the professional, this reference work discusses, in Part 1, the consumers' need for information on health. Part 2 is an annotated list of health-related bibliographies. Part 3 provides critical annotations of over 700 medical titles. Included are lists of resource organizations, films, pamphlets, and distributors.

455. Sell, Irene L. Dying and Death: An Annotated Bibliography. New York: Tiresias, 1977. 114p.
The author has annotated articles, books, and audiovisual materials dealing with the emotional, psycho-social, and interpersonal aspects of dying.

456. Sharma, Prakash C. Health Services: A Selected Research Bibliography. Monticello, Ill.: Council of Planning Librarians, 1974. 15p.
The author has collected nearly 200 selected references on

health services, including social services, published between 1940 and 1972. The bibliography is divided into two parts: a list of books and a list of periodicals.

457. Sharma, Prakash C. Medical Social Work: A Selected Bibliographic Research Guide, Part One (1950-1964). Monticello, Ill.: Vance Bibliographies, 1978. 10p.
Sharma's publication is a retrospective bibliography of 125 books and articles on medical social work. The work is divided into two sections. The first lists books, and the second journal articles.

458. Sharma, Prakash C. Medical Social Work: A Selected Bibliographic Research Guide, Part Two (1965-1975). Monticello, Ill.: Vance Bibliographies, 1978. 8p.
A continuation of Part 1, this bibliography lists 100 articles and books published between 1965 and 1975 on medical social work. The books and articles are listed separately.

459. Ticky, Monique. Behavioral Science Techniques: An Annotated Bibliography for Health Professionals. New York: Praeger, 1975. 132p.
This is a comprehensive bibliography on behavioral science techniques.

460. Ticky, Monique, editor. Health Care Teams: An Annotated Bibliography. New York: Praeger, 1974. 177p.
This publication provides an in-depth guide to the literature on health care teams.

461. U. S. Health Services Administration. Comprehensive Bibliography on Health Maintenance Organizations: 1970-1973. Rockville, Md.: Bureau of Community Health Services, 1974. 96p. HE20.5110:H34/2/970-73.
This bibliography was compiled for hospital administrators, medical social workers, and physicians involved in managment of care delivery systems. All entries appeared between 1970 and 1973.

Dictionary

462. Stedman's Medical Dictionary: A Vocabulary of Medicine and Its Allied Sciences, with Pronunciations and Derivations. 23rd ed. Baltimore: Williams and Wilkins, 1976. 1,678p.
This is one of the standard dictionaries of medical terminology. It reflects standard and current terminology for 46 specialties and subspecialties and contains 358 illustrations. The introduction includes a section on medical etymology with a comprehensive "Root Word List."

Directories

463. American Hospital Association Guide to the Health Care Field.
     Chicago: American Hospital Association, 1972- .
     Annual.
     This directory contains a list, by geographic location, of
     AHA accredited hospitals, government hospitals, and ac-
     credited long-term care facilities, with detailed informa-
     tion on each facility. Also included are statistical data on
     hospitals; international, national and local organizations
     providing health care; accredited educational programs in
     thirty different health related fields; and a buyer's guide
     to manufacturers, suppliers, and distributors of products
     used by the hospital field.

464. Annas, George J. The Rights of Hospital Patients: The Basic
     ACLU Guide to a Hospital Patient's Rights. New York:
     Sunrise/Dutton, 1975. 246p.
     Part of the Civil Liberties Union Handbook Series, this
     survey of hospital patients' rights includes bibliographical
     references and an index. Pertinent laws and legislation
     are discussed in-depth.

465. Directory of Home Health Agencies Certified as Medicare Pro-
     viders. New York: National League of Nursing, 1976.
     This directory (now out-of-print) describes agencies certi-
     fied by the Social Security Administration to provide ser-
     vices such as out-of-hospital home care by public health
     nurses, aides, social workers, etc.

466. Directory of Rural Health Care Programs. Washington, D. C. :
     Office of the Secretary, Department of Health, Educa-
     tion and Welfare, 1980. 499p. HE1.2:R88/2/979.
     This directory is a convenient guide to over 700 private
     and public organizations located in rural areas or serving
     rural populations and offering health care services. The
     organizations are alphabetical by state and, within state,
     by city or place. Information collected for each entry in-
     cludes name and address, county, service, contact person,
     type of program, ownership, total number of physicians,
     and number of persons served, sources of financial support,
     number of users, and fees.

467. A Guide to Planning, Organizing, Administering a Homemaker-
     Home Health Aide Service. New York: National Home-
     Caring Council, 1979. 250p.
     A looseleaf format, this publication discusses techniques
     for establishing and administering a homemaker and health
     aide service agency. The appendixes include a bibliography,
     a glossary, and sample forms that are mentioned in the
     text.

468. The Health Care Directory. Oradell, N. J. : Medical Econom-
     ics, 1977. 1,200p.

This directory provides information on thousands of individuals, organizations, agencies, companies, foundations, etc., that are involved in health services. The entries are arranged in 60 subject categories ranging from adoption information, employment services, hospitals, and social services to volunteer work opportunities. There is no index.

469. Health Organizations of the United States, Canada, and Internationally. College Park, Md.: P.W. Associates, 1961- . Irregular.
This publication provides information on 1,300 voluntary associations, professional societies, and nongovernmental groups concerned with health and related fields. Information on each organization includes address, officers, purposes, finances, programs, publications, prizes and awards, meeting dates, and affiliates. There is a subject index of all organizations listed.

470. Kruzas, Anthony T., editor. Medical and Health Information Directory. Detroit: Gale, 1977. 664p.
Arranged in 32 sections, this reference book provides an annotated guide to national and international organizations, state and regional associations (including social work), federal government agencies, foundations, health maintenance organizations, poison control centers, abstracts and indexes, and computerized information systems. Many of the sections have indexes. A companion volume, Health Services Directory (Gale, 1981), lists clinics, centers, and services in 33 areas of national and social concern.

471. Medicare/Medicaid Directory of Medical Facilities.... Washington, D.C.: Health Standards/Quality Bureau, Health Care Financing Administration, 1969- . Irregular. HE22.202:M46.
This is a directory of names and addresses of all medical facilities that participate as suppliers and/or providers of service to Title XVIII, Medicare-Medicaid Health Insurance for the Aged and Disabled, and Title XIX, Medical Assistance Program. Hospitals, nursing homes, long-term care units with skilled nursing staff, home health agencies with skilled nursing help, and physical therapy units are included.

472. National Health Directory. Washington, D.C.: Science and Health, 1977- . Annual.
The National Health Directory contains a list of U.S. congressmen and senators dealing with health legislation, key congressional staff concerned with health, state health officials, and regional health officials. Information given for each individual includes name, title, address, and phone; for senators and congressman, a short biographical sketch is added. It is organized into nine sections: Table of Contents, Agency Index, Congressional Name Index,

Congressional Full Committees and Their Subcommittees
Dealing with Health Matters, Congressional Delegations,
Federal Agencies, Federal Officials, Regional Officials,
and City and County Health Officials.

Manuals

473. Manual on Hospital Chaplaincy. Chicago: American Hospital
       Association, 1970. 96p.
       The Manual on Hospital Chaplaincy sets forth the essentials
       of a hospital chaplaincy program.

474. Quality and Quantity Assurance for Social Workers in Health
       Care: A Training Manual. Chicago: American Hospi-
       tal Association, 1980. 96p.
       This manual sets forth "ways that social workers can
       measure and evaluate the quality (effectiveness) and quan-
       tity (efficiency) of services to patients." Work sheets for
       the audit process are included.

Standards

475. Development of Professional Standards Review for Hospital
       Social Work. Chicago: American Hospital Association,
       1976. 60p.
       Developed by participants in a conference on hospital so-
       cial work, these standards define the role of social work
       in hospitals. Participation in peer and practice review
       are also described.

476. Organizing for Health Care: A Tool for Change. Boston:
       Beacon, 1974. 249p.
       This catalog describes community organizations working
       in the fields of health care, mental health, and drug abuse.

477. Physicians' Desk Reference to Pharmaceutical Specialties and
       Biologicals. Oradell, N.J.: Medical Economics, 1947-.
       Annual.
       This reference book gives descriptions of drugs by drug
       manufacturers. The 34th edition (1980) is arranged in
       nine sections: Manufacturer's Index, Product Name Index,
       Product Classification Section, Generic and Chemical Name
       Index, Product Information Section, Diagnostic Product In-
       formation, Poison Control Centers, and Guide to Manage-
       ment of Drug Overdose.

Encyclopedia

478. Clark, Randolph L., Jr., and Russell W. Cumley, compilers
       and editors. The Book of Health: A Medical Encyclo-

pedia for Everyone. 3rd ed. New York: Van Nostrand
Reinhold, 1973. 992p.
One of the standard medical reference works, this encyclopedia contains descriptions of all major human diseases,
the physiology and structure of organs, and treatments
usually prescribed by physicians.

Handbook

479. Essentials of Social Work Programs in Hospitals. Chicago:
American Hospital Association, 1971. 48p.
This pamphlet outlines for hospital administrators and social workers the administrative responsibilities involved in
planning, financing, staffing, and directing a hospital social work program.

Standards

480. Development of Professional Standards Review for Hospital Social Work. Chicago: American Hospital Association,
1976. 52p.
This volume, a result of a conference held January 18-21,
1976, at Bedford, Texas, defines professional standards
for hospital social workers and formulates guidelines for
peer review. There is a glossary.

481. Standards for Homemakers-Home Health Aide Services. New
York: National Council for Homemaker Services, 1965.
48p.
Addenda to the Standards was published in 1969. See also
Child Welfare League of America, Child Welfare League
of America Standards for Homemaker Service for Children
(New York: The League, 1959).

M. MENTAL HEALTH

Bibliographies and Bibliographic Guides

482. Berlin, Irving N., editor. Bibliography of Child Psychiatry
and Child Mental Health. New York: Human Sciences,
1976. 508p.
An update of Berlin's 1963 bibliography, the volume is a
reading list on child psychiatry for psychiatrists and social workers. All entries are annotated. The main section of the bibliography is followed by a selected list of
films. There are subject and author indexes.

483. Brown, Daniel G. Behavior Modification in Child, School,

and Family Mental Health: An Annotated Bibliography
on Applications with Parents and Teachers and in Marriage and Family Counseling. Champaign, Ill.: Research Press, 1972. 105p.
This publication contains abstracts of books and articles
on behavior therapy and the care and treatment of mentally
handicapped children.

484. Froelich, Robert E., editor. Film and Reviews in Psychiatry,
Psychology and Mental Health: A Descriptive and Eval-
uative Listing of Educational and Instructional Films.
Ann Arbor, Mich.: Pierian, 1971. 142p.
This bibliography lists and reviews 123 films on mental
health, giving information on year of production, whether
in color or black-and-white, sound or silent, title, and
length. A description of contents and critique of the film
are included. There are subject, distributor, type-
of-film, and reviewer indexes and a cross-index of reviews and reviewers.

485. Goelho, George V., editor. Mental Health and Social Change:
An Annotated Bibliography. Rockville, Md.: National
Institute of Mental Health, 1972. 458p. S/N1724-0249.
This multidisciplinary book is an annotated list of 730
readings drawn from over 1,000 journals and books published between 1967 and 1970. The entries are subdivided
into five sections: Biologically Oriented Approaches, Behavioral and Social Sciences, Studies in Life-Cycle: Tran-
sitions, Situational and Environmental Crises, Group Dis-
Orders and Social Stress, and Remedial Approaches to Improve Human Services.

486. Greenberg, Bette. How to Find Out in Psychiatry: A Guide
to Sources of Mental Health Information. Elmsford,
N.Y.: Pergamon, 1978. 113p.
Intended for students of psychiatry as well as Social Service professionals, the guide provides an overview of research techniques and information sources in psychiatry.
The book is arranged in 12 subject-oriented chapters (directories, mental health statistics, drugs, etc.). Supplementary material includes a list of nearly 80 classic
works in psychiatric literature, with annotations.

487. Neher, Jack, editor. Current Audio-visuals for Mental Health
Education. 2nd ed. Chicago: Marquis, 1979. 131p.
The editor has compiled reviews which originally appeared
in the Mental Health Materials Center quarterly newsletter
Sneak Previews, Current Audio-visuals. The reviews include notes on contents, treatment, potential use, and evaluation. The materials are found under 21 subject headings ranging from abortion to adoption to nursing homes
to women's abuse.

488. Padilla, Amado M. , and Paul Arnada. Latino Mental Health:
Bibliography and Abstracts. Rockville, Md. : National
Institute of Mental Health, 1974. 288p. S/N1724-00316.
There are over 490 abstracts on the psychological and
mental health of the Spanish surnamed, Spanish speaking,
or people of Spanish origin in the United States. The subject index completes the work. This publication supplements Latino Mental Health: A Review of the Literature,
by Amado M. Padilla and Rene A. Ruiz (Rockville, Md. :
National Institute of Mental Health, 1973).

489. Reducing Racism in Mental Health Institutes and Delivery Systems: A Selected Bibliography. Washington, D. C. :
National Association of Social Workers, 1975. 3p.
This is a bibliography on reducing racism in social services agencies.

490. Selective Guide to Materials for Mental Health and Family
Life Education. New York: Mental Health Materials
Center, 1976. 947p.
This volume contains evaluations of books, pamphlets,
films, and audiovisuals on mental health. Subject areas
covered include alcoholism, drug abuse, suicide and crisis
intervention, developmental disabilities, and mental illness. A final section is devoted to additional reference
sources.

491. U. S. Mental Health Materials Center. A Selective Guide to
Materials for Mental Health and Family Life Education.
Northfield, Ill. : Perennial Education, 1972. 841p.
This lists reviews of governmental and nongovernmental
educational publications and films on mental health, family
life, alcoholism, drug abuse, and suicide prevention.

492. Yarvis, Richard M. , compiler. The Resource Guide for Mental Health. Sacramento, Calif. : Pyramid Systems,
1979. 342p.
This work contains over 5,000 references relating to mental health program design, program implementation, and
preventive and educational techniques. The guide has been
organized into 13 major sections and 77 minor subsections.
Entries are not annotated.

Dictionary

493. Baxter, James W. Definitions for Use in Mental Health Information Systems. Rockville, Md. : National Institute
of Mental Health, 1980. 49p. S/N917-024-00972-5.
This dictionary defines terms and concepts used in mental
health.

Directories

494. Mental Health Directory. Rockville, Md. : National Institute
of Mental Health, 1964- . Irregular. FS2. 22/49:964.
Compiled by the National Clearinghouse for Mental Health,
this publication covers regional mental health offices of
the Department of Health and Human Services, state and
territorial mental health authorities, state hospitals, state
mental health services, voluntary mental health associations, self-help organizations for mental health, and national
mental health agencies. For each organization, information includes services, staffing, and programs. A list of
other sources of mental health information is found at the
end of the volume.

495. Mental Health Services Information and Referral Directory.
Thousand Oaks, Calif. : Ready Reference, 1978.
4 vols.
Four regional directories describe the services of counseling centers, psychiatric hospitals, residential treatment
centers, and clinics. Also listed are state mental health
authorities, regional alcohol and substance abuse offices
of the Health and Human Services Department, voluntary
mental health associations, self-help organizations, and
others.

496. National Directory of Hispanic Professionals and Human Ser-
vices in Mental Health Organizations. Washington, D. C. :
National Coalition of Hispanic Mental Health and Human
Services, 1977/78- . Biennial.
This directory lists 75 mental health community programs
and 1,250 Hispanic social service professionals.

497. The National Directory of Mental Health: A Guide to Adult Out-
Patient Mental Facilities and Services Throughout the
United States. New York: Wiley, 1979- . Irregular.
Compiled by Neal-Schuman Publishers, this nationwide
directory includes 5,600 community mental health centers,
hospitals, private facilities, clinics, and support groups
with information on types of services and therapies, staff,
forms of referral, fees, and waiting time. An index to
facilities and an index to services and therapies conclude
the work.

498. National Institute of Mental Health. Directory [of] Federally
Funded Community Mental Health Centers. Washington,
D. C. : U. S. Government Printing Office, 1978. 64p.
HE20. 8102. C73/977/erratum.
The directory lists names, addresses, and directors of
community mental health centers receiving federal funds.
Updated biennially, it also indicates the kinds of mental
health programs being funded through federal assistance.

Encyclopedia

499. Goldenson, Robert M. The Encyclopedia of Human Behavior:
     Psychology, Psychiatry, and Mental Health. Garden
     City, N. Y. : Doubleday, 1970. 2 vols.
     This encyclopedia surveys the entire spectrum of mental
     health, psychology, and psychiatry. The 1,000 entries
     range from short essays on terms to long essays on con-
     cepts, theories, and treatment techniques often supported
     by case histories. There are two indexes, one analytical
     and the other categorical. Brief biographies of famous
     psychiatrists and psychologists are included.

Guidelines

500. Cooper, Myles. Guidelines for a Minimum Statistical and
     Accounting System for Community Mental Health Centers.
     Rockville, Md. : National Institute of Mental Health,
     1973. 133p. HE20:8110:C7.
     This publication outlines the basics of an accounting sys-
     tem for small community mental health centers.

Handbooks

501. Amary, Issam B. The Rights of the Mentally Retarded--De-
     velopmentally Disabled to Treatment and Education.
     Springfield, Ill. : Thomas, 1980. 196p.
     Amary does an in-depth survey of the laws governing in-
     sanity and mental health in the 50 states and the U. S.
     territories. See also Bruce Ennis, The Rights of Mental
     Patients (Avon, 1978), and James B. Jacobs, Individual
     Rights and Institutional Authority: Prisons, Mental Hospi-
     tals, Schools, and Military: Cases and Materials (Bobbs-
     Merrill, 1979).

502. Heck, Edward T. , and others. A Guide to Mental Health Ser-
     vices. Pittsburgh: University of Pittsburgh Press,
     1973. 139p.
     This volume discusses the basic concepts of mental health,
     diagnostic labeling, professional training of practitioners,
     and treatment. Mental health facilities and sources for
     further information on mental health are included in the
     appendix.

Standards

503. Standards: Psychiatric-Mental Health Nursing Practice. Kan-
     sas City, Mo. : American Nurses' Associations, 1973.
     6p.

Developed by the American Nurses' Association Executive Committee and the Standards Committee of the Division on Psychiatric Mental Health Nursing Practice, this volume sets forth basic standards for psychiatric nursing.

Yearbook and Almanac

504. Allen, Robert D., editor. Mental Health Almanac. New York: Garland, 1978. 415p.
    The almanac covers mental health issues, graduate programs in mental health, and professional and service organizations.

505. Norback, Judith. The Mental Health Yearbook/Directory, 1979-80. New York: Van Nostrand Reinhold, 1979. 781p.
    The directory presents material on aging, alcoholism, drug abuse authorities, the rights of mental patients, halfway houses, and guidelines for research in psychology. The book contains names, addresses, descriptions, and explanations of various programs, agencies, and facilities to which people can turn for assistance. A large section is devoted to a state-by-state listing of mental health vocational guidance. Plans are underway to update the yearbook periodically.

N. MENTAL RETARDATION

Abstracts

506. Mental Retardation Abstracts. Bethesda, Md.: National Institute of Mental Health, 1964- . Irregular. FS2.22/52.
    This index includes abstracts of books and journal articles concerned with the medical, developmental, and treatment aspects of mental retardation. Separate sections are devoted to the training and role of social service professionals who work with the mentally retarded.

Bibliography

507. Segal, S. S., compiler. Mental Handicap: A Select Annotated Bibliography. Windsor, England: National Foundation for Educational Research in England and Wales, 1972. 47p.
    This volume covers some 229 British and U.S. items-- books, articles, research reports, government studies-- published between 1958 and 1971, with short annotations.

The entries are organized by author in alphabetical order.
At the end of the book there is a comprehensive subject
index to the entries.

Directories

508. Alperin, Stanley, and Melvin Alperin, editors. Directory of
     Inpatient Facilities for the Mentally Retarded. Miami:
     U.S. Directory Service, 1976. 114p.
     Arranged alphabetically by state, this computer printout
     lists 1,343 facilities serving the mentally retarded, with
     information on the name, location, and admission policies
     of each facility. This is a reprint of the National Center
     for Health Statistics Directory of Inpatient Facilities for
     the Mentally Retarded.

509. Friedman, Paul. The Rights of Mentally Retarded Persons:
     The Basic ACLU Guide for the Mentally Retarded Per-
     sons' Rights. New York: Avon, 1976. 186p.
     This publication discusses the legal aspects of insanity and
     mental health in the United States.

510. Jacobs, Angeline M., Judith K. Larsen, and Claudette A.
     Smith. Handbook for Job Placement of Mentally Re-
     tarded Workers: Training, Opportunities, and Career
     Areas. 3rd ed. New York: Garland/STPM, 1979.
     326p.
     First published in 1960 under the title Guide to Jobs for
     the Mentally Retarded, this book deals with employing the
     mentally retarded. Chapter VI contains job profiles, job
     descriptions, and job activities.

Standards

511. Standards for Community Agencies Serving Persons with Men-
     tal Retardation and Other Developmental Disabilities.
     Chicago: Joint Commission on Accreditation of Hospi-
     tals and Accreditation Council for Facilities for the Men-
     tal Retarded, 1973. 154p.
     This book outlines the essentials of a model community
     mental retardation agency.

512. Standards for Residential Facilities for the Mental Retarded.
     Chicago: Joint Commission on Accreditation of Hospi-
     tals and Accreditation Council for Facilities for the
     Mental Retarded, 1973. 159p.
     This publication summarizes the minimum standards for
     residential facilities for the mentally retarded.

O. POVERTY

Abstracts

513. Human Resources Abstracts: An International Information Service. Beverly Hills, Calif.: Sage, 1975- . Quarterly.
Each issue contains 200 to 300 abstracts from a variety of disciplines concerned with human, social, and manpower problems. All aspects of poverty, from legal rights and assistance for the poor to income and social mobility, are surveyed. The fourth quarterly issue contains the annual author and subject indexes. Earlier titles for this publication were Poverty and Human Resources (1970-1974) and Poverty and Human Resources Abstracts (1966-1969).

Bibliographies

514. Cameron, Colin, compiler. Attitudes of the Poor and Attitudes toward the Poor. Madison: Institute for Research on Poverty, University of Wisconsin, 1975. 184p.
This is an annotated, classified bibliography of books and articles on the subject of poverty in the U.S. Entries cover the period 1965 to 1973. The volume contains thorough author and subject indexes.

515. Childers, Thomas. The Information-Poor in America. Metuchen, N.J.: Scarecrow, 1975. 182p.
The book is divided into two sections. The first discusses the information needs of the poor; the second is a bibliography of 725 documents, books, pamphlets, articles, and government documents related to the information needs and patterns of behavior of the poor. The entries are arranged alphabetically, with asterisks indicating the most important works.

516. Dunmore, Charlotte. Poverty, Participation, Protest, Power and Black Americans: A Selected Bibliography for Use in Social Work Education. New York: Council on Social Work Education, 1970. 67p.
This is a selected bibliography of books, articles, and government publications on problems relating to black Americans. There are sections on education, housing, economics, mental health, family life, and social work.

517. Gregson, J. Randolph, II. Skid Row: A Wide-Ranging Bibliography. Monticello, Ill.: Council of Planning Librarians, 1977. 25p.
Gregson has compiled a list of books and articles on legal, medical, psychological, and sociological aspect of Skid Row, with particular attention to alcoholics.

518. Tompkins, Dorothy Louise Culver. Poverty in the United

States During the Sixties: A Bibliography. Berkeley: University of California, Institute of Governmental Studies, 1970. 542p.

Citations from many subject areas, including social welfare, sociology, public administration, and law, are arranged by broad subject areas in this lengthy bibliography. There are subject and author indexes.

519. White, Anthony G. Skid Row as Urban Subcommunity: A Bibliography. Monticello, Ill.: Council of Planning Librarians, 1974. 7p.

This bibliography focuses on sociological studies of Skid Row as an urban subcommunity.

Chronology

520. Grønbjerg, Kirsten, and others. Poverty and Social Change. Chicago: University of Chicago Press, 1978. 248p.

The last section of this book contains a 34p. chronology of legislation, publications, and other important events connected with welfare and poverty in the United States and Great Britain from A.D. 800 to 1974.

P. PUBLIC ASSISTANCE

Data Book

521. Campbell, Toby H., and Marc Bendick, Jr. A Public Assistance Data Book. Washington, D.C.: Urban Institute, 1977. 344p.

This book contains 104 statistical tables on public welfare assistance published between 1974-1976. The statistics have been arranged under five Chapters: Characteristics of Public Assistance Clients, Public Assistance Eligibility and Benefit Policies, Characteristics of Public Assistance Staff, Public Assistance Program Operations, and Public Assistance Program Performance.

Directories

522. Catalog of Federal Domestic Assistance. Washington, D.C.: U.S. Office of Management and Budget, 1971- . Semiannual. PrEx10.2:P94/(date).

Prepared by the Office of Management and Budget, the catalog is a comprehensive list of all domestic programs involving federal grants and financial assistance administered by federal agencies. The entries explain the nature and purpose of programs, eligibility requirements, printed material available, and how to apply for assistance.

523. The Public Welfare Directory. Chicago: American Public
        Welfare Association, 1940- . Annual.
        This directory lists all federal, state, and local public
        welfare agencies in the United States and Canada. The
        section on federal agencies describes their organization,
        administration, and programs. For each state there is
        indicated which agencies take adminstrative responsibility
        for public welfare and where to write for information on
        assistance and birth and death records. Also included are
        the addresses of related state agencies and the directors
        and addresses for all county departments of social ser-
        vices. The appendix has a table on state residence re-
        quirements for assistance.

Handbook

524. Spindler, Arthur. Public Welfare. New York: Human Sci-
        ences, 1979. 513p.
        The author, a former Department of Health, Education
        and Welfare Planning and Evaluation Officer, has produced
        an exhaustive study of public welfare programs, organiza-
        tions, financing, staffing, and personnel administration.
        The volume is fully indexed and referenced and contains
        47 charts, figures, and tables.

Q. SEXUALITY

Abstracts

525. Perkins, Barbara B. Adolescent Birth Planning and Sexuality:
        Abstracts of the Literature. New York: Child Wel-
        fare League of America, 1974. 75p.
        Perkins has abstracted 101 articles on teenage pregnancy,
        adolescent abortion, and adolescent sexuality.

Bibliographies

526. Astin, Helen S. , and others, editors. Sex Roles: A Research
        Bibliography. Rockville, Md. : National Institute of
        Mental Health; distr. Washington, D. C. : U. S. Govern-
        ment Printing Office, 1975. 352p. HE20. 8113:Se9.
        This annotated bibliography provides access to descriptive
        studies of sex roles. The entries are organized into six
        subject areas: Sex Differences, Development of Sex Dif-
        ferences and Sex Roles, Specialized Sex Roles in Institu-
        tional Settings, Cross-Cultural Overviews of the Status of
        the Sexes, and Reviews and Theoretical Expositions. Au-
        thor and subject indexes conclude the bibliography.

527. Brewer, Joan Scherer, and Rod W. Wright, compilers. Sex Research Bibliographies from the Institute for Sex Research. Phoenix: Oryx, in association with Neal-Schuman, 1979. 212p.
    This work, containing more than 4,000 entries, is a collection of the most frequently requested bibliographies from the Institute for Sex Research. No annotations are provided, but there are two indexes: subject and author. The entries are arranged in 11 broad categories.

528. Bullough, Vern L., and others. An Annotated Bibliography of Homosexuality. New York: Garland, 1976. 468p.
    A continuation of Volume 1, this fully annotated bibliography cites 7,218 books and articles on all aspects of homosexuality--male and female homosexuality, transvestism, and transsexualism. An author index and a 25p. history of the Homophile Movement (1948-1960), written by S. Licata, are included.

529. Bullough, Vern L., and others. A Bibliography on Prostitution. New York: Garland, 1977. 419p.
    This detailed bibliography on the subject of prostitution contains 5,494 entries in 20 subject categories.

530. A Gay Bibliography: Eight Bibliographies on Lesbian and Male Homosexuality. New York: Arno, 1975. 410p.
    A retrospective bibliography, this work contains eight annotated or coded bibliographies that appeared in the late 1950s and the 1960s. The last bibliography reprinted is William Parker's Homosexuality: Selected Abstracts and Bibliography (1966), which deals with sociological literature on homosexuality.

531. Parker, William. Homosexuality: A Selective Bibliography of Over 3,000 Items. Metuchen, N.J.: Scarecrow, 1971. 323p.
    Parker cites 3,188 works that appeared in academic and popular magazines, books, pamphlets, documents, theses, and dissertations on the topic of gays. Included also are over 100 court cases involving homosexual acts and a list of literary works, movies, television programs, and phonograph records dealing with homosexuality.

532. Stewart, Karen Robb, compiler and editor. Adolescent Sexuality and Teenage Pregnancy: A Selected, Annotated Bibliography with Summary Forewords. Chapel Hill: Carolina Population Center, University of North Carolina, 1976. 43p.
    Eight short essays introduce a selected annotated bibliography on sexuality and teenage pregnancy.

533. Vida, Ginny, editor. Our Right to Love: A Lesbian Resource Book. Englewood Cliffs, N.J.: Prentice-Hall, 1978. 325p.

In addition to general essays on lesbianism, this book provides practical information on where to locate health services, counseling services, and bookstores for lesbians.

Catalog

534. Sanders, Dennis. Gay Source: A Catalog for Men. New York: Coward, McCann and Geoghegan, 1977. 287p. The author gives directory-type information on homosexual periodicals, bookstores, organizations, hotlines, and other resources, plus 28 articles on various aspects of homosexuality.

R. SUICIDE

Bibliographies and Bibliographical Guides

535. Lester, David, and others, editors. Suicide: A Guide to Information Sources. Detroit: Gale, 1980. 294p. The bibliography cites articles and books on suicide. It is arranged in five parts: Sources for Locating Information and Materials on Suicide, Selected References on Theories of Suicide, Selected References on Social and Environmental Correlates of Suicide, Selected References to Psychological Correlates and Analyses of Suicide, and Selected References on Suicide Prevention.

536. Poteet, G. Howard, and Joseph C. Santora. Suicide: A Bibliography for Nineteen Fifty to Nineteen Seventy-Four: A Supplement to Death and Dying: A Bibliography for Nineteen Fifty to Nineteen Seventy-Four. Troy, N.Y.: Whitston, 1978. 166p. This volume covers the psychological and sociological aspects of suicide and death. A large number of books and articles from a wide range of sources are listed. The entries are not annotated.

537. Prentice, Ann E. Suicide: A Selective Bibliography of Over 2,200 Items. Metuchen, N.J.: Scarecrow, 1974. 227p. This bibliography lists 2,218 items, including articles, literary works, scholarly works, popular magazine articles, films, and tapes on suicide. Most of the works were published between 1963 and 1973. Author and subject indexes are provided.

Directory

538. Suicide Prevention and Crisis Intervention Agencies in the

United States.   Houston: American Association of Suicidology, 1977.   14p.
The AAS, an information clearinghouse on suicide prevention, collected data on about 200 suicide prevention and
crisis intervention centers through out the United States.
The directory is being updated by AAS.

Standards

539.   Motto, Jerome A., and others.   Standards for Suicide Preven-
        tion and Crisis Centers.   New York: Behavioral, 1974.
        114p.
        This official publication of the American Association of
        Suicidology discusses basics of establishing and adminis-
        tering a crisis intervention center.   The book includes a
        bibliography.

S.   WOMEN

Abstracts

540.   Women Studies Abstracts.   Rush, N.Y.:   Women Studies Ab-
        stracts, 1972- .   Quarterly, with yearly cumulated
        index.
        This service abstracts books, articles, and reports on sex
        roles, sexuality, family, mental and physical health, preg-
        nancy, family planning, childbirth, and abortion.   In ad-
        dition to the abstract section, each issue contains one or
        more interpretative bibliographic essays and a detailed
        subject index.

Bibliographies and Bibliographic Guides

541.   Ballou, Patricia K.   Women: A Bibliography of Bibliographies.
        Boston: Hall, 1980.   155p.
        The bibliographies listed in this book date from 1970 through
        1979 and are arranged by specific categories.   Bibliogra-
        phies dealing with race, age, marital status, ethnic and
        racial groups, marriage, and family are grouped together
        as subsections of Sociology.   Those dealing with therapy,
        counseling, teenage pregnancy, childbirth, fertility, and
        contraception are listed under the subsection of Psychology,
        Health, and Reproduction.   There are cross-references
        and an index.

542.   Cromwell, Phyllis E., editor.   Woman and Mental Health:
        Selected Annotated References, 1970-1973.   Rockville,
        Md.:   National Institute of Mental Health, 1974.   247p.
        DHEW publication no. (ADM)75-142.

Cromwell has compiled an annotated guide to 810 references on women and mental health drawn from journals, books, and audiovisual sources published between 1970 and 1973. The entries are classified. Some of the topics covered are abortion, aging, divorce, lesbianism, motherhood, rape, roles, sexuality and sexual development, and widowhood. An author index completes the bibliography.

543. Howard, Pamela. Wife Beating: A Selected Bibliography. San Diego, Calif. : Current Bibliography Series, 1978. 57p.
Over 140 government documents, films, books, pamphlets, and articles on wife beating are listed in this annotated bibliography. The last part of the book describes shelters and agencies and the services they provide to battered wives.

544. Hughes, Marja Matich. The Sexual Barrier: Legal, Medical, Economic and Social Aspects of Sex Discrimination. Enl. and rev. ed. Washington, D.C. : Hughes, 1977. 843p.
International in coverage, this bibliography annotates 8,000 items concerned with women. Specific aspects of interest to social workers are: aging, child care, social security, child custody, marriage contracts, family violence, lesbianism, minority women, maternity laws, and other legal issues of interest to women. Most of the material was published between 1960 and 1975. The entries are arranged into 17 chapters.

545. Kemmer, Elizabeth Jane. Rape and Rape Related Issues: An Annotated Bibliography. New York: Garland, 1977. 174p.
This bibliography provides access to 350 books and articles on rape published between 1965 and 1976. The book includes a short subject index.

546. National Clearinghouse for Drug Abuse Information. Women and Drugs: An Annotated Bibliography. Rockville, Md. : National Institute on Drug Abuse, 1975. 62p. HE20. 8211/2:4.
The references included in this bibliography span the period from 1937 through June 1975. The entries are organized into four sections: General Articles, Women and Narcotics, Women and Psychotherapeutic Drug Use, and Women and Alcohol. These sections are in turn subdivided under such headings as treatment, service delivery, and psychological aspects.

547. Oakes, Elizabeth H. , and Kathleen E. Sheldon. Guide to Social Science Resources in Women's Studies. Santa Barbara, Calif. : ABC-Clio, 1978. 162p.
Most of the works included are scholarly. Sections of in-

terest to social service professionals are Marriage and
Motherhood, Sex Roles, Female Personality and Sexuality,
and Sex Differences. All references are annotated.

548. Walstedt, Joyce Jennings. The Psychology of Women: A
Partially Annotated Bibliography. Pittsburgh: Know,
1972. 76p.
This is a partially annotated bibliography on the psychology
of women. Another extensive review is Julia Sherman's
On the Psychology of Women (Springfield, Ill.: Thomas,
1971).

549. White, Anthony G. Rape: An Urban Crime?: A Selected
Bibliography. Monticello, Ill.: Council of Planning
Librarians, 1977. 15p.
The author has selected approximately 150 items on rape.
Most of the books and articles were published in the 1960s
and early 1970s.

Directories

550. Boston Women's Collective. The New York Women's Yellow
Pages. 1978/79 ed. New York: St. Martin, 1978.
The volume is a guide to services available to women in
New York and includes information on child care, profes-
sional counseling, rape, women's groups, and health care.
The Boston Women's Collective has prepared a yellow pages
for the Boston area.

551. Warrior, Betsy. Battered Women Directory. 8th ed. Cambridge, Mass.: Warrior, 1981. 200p.
Formerly titled Working on Wife Abuse, this directory lists
more than 2,000 refuges for battered women. The book
also has a list of publications and films relevant to battered women and recommendations on establishing refuges
for battered women and programs for battering men.

Guide

552. Alexander, Shana. State by State Guide to Women's Legal
Rights. Los Angeles: Wollstonecraft, 1975. 156p.
This book is a state-by-state guide on women's rights in
respect to marriage, divorce, children, abortion, rape,
widowhood, etc. A glossary of terms completes the publication. The American Civil Liberties Union has published a series on the rights of various oppressed groups
--prisoners, mental patients, students, minorities, the
poor, and women. The ACLU book on women is The Rights
of Women: The Basic ACLU Guide to Woman's Rights
(New York: Sunrise/Dutton, 1973).

Handbooks

553. Beere, Carol A. Women and Women's Issues: A Handbook
of Tests and Measures. San Francisco: Jossey-Bass,
1979. 560p.
This volume describes and evaluates over 230 selected
tests and measures relevant for the study of women. Information for each test includes title, author, date of first
use of the test, administration and scoring, data on re-
liability and validity, and characteristics of past and potential respondents' sources.

554. Francis, Philip. Legal Status of Women. 2nd ed. Dobbs
Ferry, N. Y.: Oceana, 1978. 122p.
The legal status of women is explored in relation to marriage, abortion, property rights, divorce, employment,
and crime.

555. Grimstad, Kirsten, and Susan Rennie, editors. The New Woman's Survival Sourcebook. New York: Knopf, 1975.
245p.
A useful source of information on women's issues, this
book covers health and child care, employment, women's
literature and publishing, abortion, family planning, sexuality, etc.

Almanac

556. Women's Rights Almanac. Gaithersburg, Md.: Elizabeth Cady
Stanton, 1974. 512p.
This is an encyclopedic collection of facts, issues, per-
sonalities, and events of concern to women. It includes
health services, women's organizations, elected women
officials, bibliographies, legislation affecting women, and
information on the women's movement. The book lists
over 1,500 local, state, and national women's service and
special interest groups. A similar book is Kathryn Paul-
sein's Woman's Almanac: 12 How-to-Hand-Books-in-One
(New York: Lippincott, 1976).

5. SERVICE METHODS

A. ADMINISTRATION

Abstracts

557. <u>Journal of Human Services Abstracts.</u> Rockville, Md.: Project Share, January 1976- . Irregular. HE1.50.
Project Share, a federally operated clearinghouse for improving the management of human services, publishes abstracts of reports and studies on subjects of interest to social work administrators. The abstracts are arranged in alphabetical order by title, and subjects are classified into about 100 categories. Most of the reports and studies are available on order from Project Share.

Bibliographies

558. Lorenson, Donna, and Dwight F. Davis. <u>Evaluation of Social Service Programs: An Annotated and Unannotated Bibliography.</u> Norman: University of Oklahoma Government Research, 1977. 167p.
Lorenson and Davis have compiled a bibliography of articles, reports, and books on evaluation, needs assessment, and planning.

559. Patti, Rino, compiler. <u>Management Practice in Social Welfare: An Annotated Bibliography.</u> New York: Council on Social Work Education, 1976. 107p.
This volume lists the literature on social welfare administration/management. Appendixes contain a bibliography of doctoral dissertations in social work on the subject of management practices. Selected journals relating to administration and management are also listed.

560. Raeburn, Michele, compiler. <u>Administrative Supervision: An Annotated Bibliography.</u> Los Angeles: Curriculum Development Project, School of Social Work, University of Southern California, 1977. 7p.
Raeburn's bibliography lists both books and articles on administrative supervision in social work agencies.

561. White, Anthony G. <u>Evaluation of Social Programs: A Selected</u>

Bibliography. Monticello, Ill.: Council of Planning
Librarians, 1977. 8p.
The Council of Planning Librarians bibliography provides
a selective coverage to the literature on evaluation methods
of social programs.

562. White, Anthony G. Local Public Service Site Selection: A
Bibliography. Monticello, Ill.: Council of Planning
Librarians, 1975. 6p.
This bibliography lists books and articles on site selection
for social service agencies.

Guides

563. Budgeting: A Guide for United Ways and Not-for-Profit Human
Service Organizations. Alexandria, Va.: United Way
of America Systems, 1975. 55p.
This book offers general guidelines for social agencies
wishing to improve their budgetary procedures.

564. The Family Service Executive: Selection and Performance
Appraisal: Guide Material for an Agency Board of Di-
rectors. New York: Family Service Association of
America, 1974. 54p.
It includes supplement #71/1-45, Termination of Employ-
ment.

565. Guide for Board Organization in Social Agencies. Rev. ed.
New York: Child Welfare League of America, 1975.
36p.
A revision of the 1951 and 1963 editions this volume presents "a description of sound practice and offers a frame-
work for agencies with varied patterns and services to
study their own operations in order to maintain the vigor
of their leadership." There is a bibliography at the end
of the volume.

Handbooks and Manuals

566. An Accounting Manual for Voluntary Social Welfare Organizations. New York: Child Welfare League of America,
1971.
Prepared jointly by the CWLA, Family Service Association
of America, and Travelers Aid Association of America,
this manual explains the procedures for preparing financial
reports that conform to the Standards of Accounting and Financial Reporting for Voluntary Health and Welfare Organizations.

567. The Board Member of a Social Agency: Responsibilities and
Functions. New York: Child Welfare League of America, 1957. 82p.

Board members and social agency executives discuss major aspects of establishing and administering a social
agency.

568. Handbook on Private Practice of Social Work. Washington,
         D. C.: National Association of Social Workers, 1974.
         63p.
         This work contains information on private practice, spe-
         cial problems of casework in private practice, standards
         of ethics and competence, state licensing of private prac-
         tice, and managing expenses and fees.

Review

569. Evaluation Studies: Review. Beverly Hills, Calif.: Sage,
         1976- . Annual.
         Each issue contains a collection of papers on the subject
         of evaluation. Chapters are arranged according to policy
         areas, such as social services, labor, housing, crime
         and justice, and methodology.

Standards

570. Standards of Accounting and Financial Reporting for Voluntary
         Health and Welfare Organizations. Alexandria, Va.:
         United Way of America, 1975. 135p.
         Prepared jointly by the National Health Council, National
         Voluntary Health and Social Welfare Organizations, and
         United Way of America, the Standards supersedes the 1964
         edition.

B.   COMMUNITY ORGANIZATION

Bibliographies

571. Kline, Paula. Urban Needs: A Bibliography and Directory
         for Community Resource Centers. Metuchen, N. J.:
         Scarecrow, 1978. 257p.
         Kline's book is both a bibliography and a directory to com-
         munity services, economic development, employment, hous-
         ing, legal services, health care, and cultural activities.
         Chapters are divided by subject and contain fully annotated,
         alphabetically arranged entries. In addition, there are au-
         thor, title, and subject indexes and an appendix of pub-
         lishers' addresses.

572. Poole, Dennis. Rural Welfare: Educators and Practitioners.
         New York: Praeger, 1981. 317p.

This is a comprehensive annotated bibliography of rural social welfare for social work educators and practitioners. The book is divided into ten chapters.

573. Zimpfer, David G., editor. Group Work in the Helping Professions: A Bibliography. Washington, D.C.: Association for Specialists in Group Work; distr. Rochester, N.Y.: The University of Rochester, 1976. 452p.
This is an annotated bibliography of journal articles, books, and pamphlets designed to provide social workers with references to information on group work, guidance, and counseling in education. The entries are divided among 75 subject categories.

Directories

574. Directory: Community Development Education and Training Programs Throughout the World. 1976 ed. Columbia, Mo.: Community Development Society, 1976. 36p.
This directory covers undergraduate, advanced, and associate degrees, as well as diplomas and certificates and short-term programs offering a concentration in community development. For each school data are provided on the program, admission requirements, fees, staff, professors, and where to write for further information.

575. Evans, Glen. The Family Circle: Guide to Self-Help. New York: Ballantine, 1979. 240p.
The core of this volume is a listing of more than 450 self-help organizations in the United States and Canada, with information on their history, goals, achievements, and organization. Organizations range from the National Ataxia Foundation to Aid for New Mothers.

576. Gartner, Alan, and Frank Riessman, compilers. A Working Guide to Self-Help Groups. New York: New Viewpoints/ Vision, 1980. 184p.
The self-help groups listed in this directory range from Abused Women's Aid in Crisis to Alcoholics Anonymous. Information on each group includes name, address, date established, description of activities, services, and current members' statements on the organization. The compilers, codirectors of the National Self-Help Clearinghouse, have written chapters on Organizing Self-Help Mutual Aid Groups and Professional Self-Help Mutual Aid Groups.

577. Service Directory of National Voluntary Health and Social Welfare Organizations. New York: National Assembly of National Voluntary Health and Social Welfare Organizations, 1971- . Biennial (even years).
This directory covers 105 organizations concerned with social welfare and health services. Entries, arranged by

type of organization (voluntary and governmental), include purposes of the organization, services offered, and how services may be obtained. There is an alphabetical index.

Handbook

578. Drezner, Stephen, and William B. McCurdy. A Planning Handbook for Voluntary Social Welfare Agencies. New York: Family Service Association of America, 1973. 224p.
This looseleaf notebook contains 18 sections outlining techniques and procedures for improved planning for voluntary social welfare agencies.

Manual

579. U. S. Community Service Administration. Citizen Participation. San Jose, Calif.: Rapids, 1978. 140p.
This book summarizes requirements for participation in federally assisted programs. Programs are listed by agency and each program is designated by a title and number assigned to it in the Catalog of Federal Domestic Assistance (item 33). Programs of the Community Service Administration, Appalachian Regional Commission, and Department of Housing and Urban Development are listed in this directory. A bibliography and glossary are found in the appendix.

C. GRANTSMANSHIP

Bibliography

580. Poverny, Linda. Grantsmanship and Fund Raising for Social Welfare Agencies: An Annotated Bibliography. Berkeley: University of California, School of Social Work, Administration Curriculum, 1977. 15p.
This bibliography covers four areas of grantsmanship and fund raising for social service professionals: Revenue Sharing, the A-95 Clearinghouse Review Process, the TC-1082 Grant Information System, and Standardization of Federal Grant Administration Procedures.

Directories

581. Annual Register of Grant Support. Orange, N. Y.: Academic Media, 1969- . Annual.
The register is a guide to grant-support programs of government agencies, foundations, and business and profes-

sional organizations. Each entry provides the organization's name, address, telephone number, purpose, and type as well as the duration of the grant and instructions for applicants. Entries are divided into ten broad subject categories, such as minorities, social sciences, and social services. There are subject, organization, program, geographic, and personnel indexes.

582. Berryman, Phillip, and others. Guide to Global Giving: A Critical Introduction to Voluntary International Aid Agencies in the United States. Philadelphia: Life Center Movement for a New Society, 1976. 59p.
The introduction provides an overview of governmental and private U. S. aid to foreign countries. Entries on overseas agencies include name, address, date of establishment, description of purpose and work, general financial data, and the composition of the board of directors, executive committee, and staff.

583. Cohen, Lilly, compiler. A National Guide to Government and Foundation Funding Sources in the Field of Aging. Garden City, N. Y.: Adelphi University Press, 1977. 174p.
This guide is divided into two separate sections: federal funding sources and private sources. Included for each federal source is name of agency, authorization, objectives, eligibility requirements, application procedures, assistance considerations, and information contacts. For the private foundations, each entry lists address, assets, emphasis, and where the money was spent. An index to government programs and an index to foundations conclude the work.

584. Foundation Center Source Book. New York: Foundation Center, 1975/76- . Biennial.
This publication is designed "to relate the needs of fund seekers to the activities of foundations and to assist foundations in making their programs known to the public." Foundations are listed alphabetically, with the following information given for each: 1) descriptive and fiscal data; 2) statement of policy, programs, and application procedures; and 3) a listing of recent grants illustrating the current programs.

585. The Foundation Directory. Irvington, N. Y.: Columbia University Press, 1960- . Biennial.
The most comprehensive source of information on grant-making foundations in the United States, the directory provides complete information on over 5,000 U. S. charitable, educational, and cultural foundations with assets over $500,000 or annual grants over $25,000. Information on each foundation includes name and address of the foundation, its purpose and activities, financial data on number of grants made, names of officers and trustees, and the name of the person to whom correspondence should be di-

rected. Foundations are listed alphabetically by state with separate indexes to the foundations by field of interest; by state and city; by donor, trustees, and administrators; and by names of foundations. The directory is kept up to date through four semiannual supplements, the Foundation Center Information Quarterly. The files are available online through Lockheed's DIALOG Information Retrieval Service.

Handbooks

586. Fulton, Lynn F., and others. Grant Writing Guide for Social Workers. Ann Arbor, Mich.: Campus, 1972. 40p. The authors have written a basic text for social workers on grant writing. Chapters include Guidelines for Completing Application Forms for Grants, Nature and Scope of Fund Raising, and Legislation Controlling Grants.

587. Lauffer, Armand. Grantsmanship. Beverly Hills, Calif.: Sage, 1977. 120p. Lauffer's book, designed for social service professionals who are seeking to acquire financial resources to support social programs, provides practical information on grant writing. Useful features are inclusion of a bibliography on grantsmanship, a list of agencies dealing with human services, and sources of information on grantsmanship.

588. Lefferts, Robert. Getting a Grant: How to Write Successful Grants Proposals. Englewood Cliffs, N.J.: Prentice-Hall, 1978. 160p. Prepared for social workers, this book covers developing a strategy, writing the proposal, getting the information and follow-up. In addition, it includes a glossary of terms and a 30p. annotated list of books, periodicals, reports, and newsletters that are available to social workers preparing proposals and locating funding sources.

589. Soroker, Gerald S. Fund Raising for Philanthropy. Pittsburgh: Pittsburgh Jewish Publications and Education Foundation, 1974. 190p. This book outlines basic information on fund raising for social workers. It is divided into two main sections. The first part includes information on why people give money, the role of the professional in relationship to the volunteer, and fund raising campaigns. The second half discusses basic community organization strategies in relationship to fund raising.

Manuals

590. Copeland, William C. Finding Federal Money for Children's

Services. New York: Child Welfare League of America, 1976. 63p.
The volume describes sources of funding for children's services, with primary emphasis on Title XX funds. Four other manuals--Obtaining Federal Money for Children's Services, Audit-Proof Contracting for Federal Money for Children's Services, Managing Federal Money for Children's Services, and A Roadmap Through Title XX--complete the series.

591. One Hundred Foundations: A Manual for Legal Services Programs Seeking Funding for Senior Citizens Projects. Los Angeles: National Senior Citizens Law Center, 1973. 61p.
Though somewhat dated, this manual lists 100 foundations that fund programs for the aging.

D. LEGAL ASPECTS OF SOCIAL WORK

Index

592. Index to Legal Periodicals. New York: H. W. Wilson in cooperation with the American Association of Law Libraries, 1908- . Monthly, with annual and triennial cumulations.
A good source for information on the legal aspects of social work, civil rights, welfare recipient rights, poverty law, etc., this is a basic author and subject index to nearly 400 legal and law-related periodicals in the United States, Canada, Great Britain, Northern Ireland, Australia, and New Zealand. Book reviews, case notes, yearbooks, annual institutes, and annual reviews are indexed in addition to the articles.

Bibliographies

593. Boston, Guy, and others. Criminal Justice and the Elderly: A Selected Bibliography. Washington, D. C.: National Council of Senior Citizens, 1979. 104p.
The book's 150 entries are organized under four areas: the Impact of Crime on Elderly, the Elderly as Victims of Consumer Fraud, Victim Assistance and Restitution, and the Involvement of Elderly in the Criminal Justice System.

594. Lewis, Mary R. "Social Policy Research: A Guide to Legal and Government Documents." Social Service Review, 50 (December 1976), 647-654.
This article summarizes the basic sources available for

doing social policy research. Emphasis is placed on basic primary source documents, such as U. S. Code Annotated (USCA), U. S. Statutes at Large, and Congressional Index.

Code

595. United States Code. 1970 ed. Washington, D. C. : U. S. Government Printing Office, 1971. Supplement, 1972- .
Y1. 2/5.
The code rearranges federal laws under 50 subject headings, called "titles." The code also serves as an index
to the U. S. Statutes at Large.

Dictionaries

596. Black's Law Dictionary. Rev. 4th ed. St. Paul, Minn. :
West, 1963. 1,882p.
The subtitle reads: "Definitions of the Terms and Phrases
of American and English Jurisprudence, Ancient and Modern." A comprehensive list of legal abbreviations is also
included.

597. Redden, Kenneth R. , and Enid L. Veron. Modern Legal Glossary. Charlottesville, Va. : Michie, 1980. 576p.
This glossary identifies legal terms and related concepts,
professional associations, government agencies, international organizations, foreign expressions, popular legal
cases, famous trials, classic law books, ancient codes,
and famous lawyers and judges.

Handbooks

598. Agostinelli, A. J. Legal Regulation of Social Work Practice.
Washington, D. C. : National Association of Social Workers,
1973. 17p.
This pamphlet surveys the legal aspects of private practice
with particular emphasis on licensing.

599. Annas, George J. The Rights of Hospital Patients: The Basic
ACLU Guide to a Hospital Patient's Rights. New York:
Sunrise/Dutton, 1975. 246p.
Part of the Civil Liberties Union Handbook, this survey
of hospital patients' rights includes bibliographical references
and index. Pertinent laws and legislation are discussed
in depth.

600. Brieland, Donald, and John Lemnon. Social Work and the
Law. St. Paul, Minn. : West, 1977. 830p.
Prepared for social workers and their clients, the book is
designed to "help social workers understand legal reasoning

and key areas of legal knowledge of importance to social workers." Arranged in five sections, it provides information on family law, poverty law, consumer law, civil rights, how to testify, and rules of evidence. Selected definitions, appendix, and index complete the volume.

601. Burgdorf, Robert L., Jr., editor. The Legal Rights of Handicapped Persons: Cases, Materials and Text. Baltimore: Brookes, 1980. 1,127p.
Designed for use in law school courses, the book covers all legal areas where the handicapped have been denied rights or benefits. Chapters include employment, access to buildings, transportation systems, freedom from residential confinement, equal access to medical services, procreation, marriage, and raising children.

602. Caulfield, Barbara. Child Abuse and the Law: A Legal Primer for Social Workers. Chicago: National Committee for Prevention of Child Abuse, 1979. 64p.
In addition to presenting an introduction to child abuse laws, the book includes information on the interpretation of child abuse laws as they affect social workers.

603. Kravse, Harry D. Family Law in a Nutshell. St. Paul, Minn.: West, 1977. 400p.
Kravse has written a concise summary of family law for social workers.

604. National Conference of Lawyers and Social Workers. Law and Social Work. Washington, D.C.: National Association of Social Workers, 1973. 64p.
This is a collection of statements on nine specific areas of interest to social workers, including adoption, child custody, confidentiality, and family court. The rights of welfare recipients are printed in the pamphlet.

605. Roberts, Joseph, and Bonnie Hawk. Legal Rights Primer for the Handicapped: In and Out of the Classroom. Novato, Calif.: Academic Therapy, 1980. 160p.
This book outlines the rights of handicapped in and out of the classroom. The book includes a summary of Section 504 and the complete text of PL94-142.

606. Shain, Henry. Legal First Aid. New York: Funk and Wagnalls, 1975. 366p.
Chapter 7 of this book provides a digest of adoption laws and a useful chart listing adoption laws of all the states.

607. Sloan, Irving J. Youth and the Law: Rights, Privileges and Obligations. 3rd ed. Dobbs Ferry, N.Y.: Oceana, 1978. 118p.
The book gives full coverage in the following areas of interest to social service professionals: Judicial System;

Youth and Ownership and Operation of Motor Vehicles; Youth and Contracts; Youth and Law of Torts; Youth, Narcotics and Alcohol; Juveniles and Criminal Justice; Youth and Marriage; Youth and Labor Law; Youth and the School; and Youth and the Environment. There is a glossary of legal terms.

608. Thomas, George, and others. The Legal Status of Adolescents. Athens, Ga.: Regional Institute of Social Welfare Research, 1980. 408p.
This report discusses the laws and court decisions on adolescents in all 50 states. Minors' consent relative to marriage, birth control and abortion, child labor laws, and the limits of juvenile court jurisdiction are some of the 47 topics treated.

Manual

609. One Hundred Foundations: A Manual for Legal Services Programs Seeking Funding for Senior Citizens Projects. Los Angeles: National Senior Citizens Law Center, 1973. 61p.
Though somewhat dated, this work lists 100 foundations that fund programs for the aging.

Standards

610. Flicker, Barbara. Standards for Juvenile Justice: A Summary and Analysis. Cambridge, Mass.: Ballinger, 1977. 276p.
This publication analyzes the Institute of Judicial Administration--American Bar Association Juvenile Justice Standards Project. There are 11 volumes in the Juvenile Justice Standards series relating to rights of minors, juvenile probation function, transfer between courts, youth service agencies, planning for juvenile justice, noncriminal behavior, monitoring, sanctions, juvenile records and information systems, dispositional procedures, and counsel for private parties.

611. A Model Licensing Act for Social Workers. Washington, D.C.: National Association of Social Workers, 1973.
This model licensing act is reprinted from Legal Regulation of Social Work Practice.

612. Standards Relating to Adjudication. Cambridge, Mass.: Ballinger, 1977. 88p.
Standards was sponsored by the Institute of Judicial Administration as part of the American Bar Association's Juvenile Justice Standards Project. Others in the series are: Standards Relating to Appeals and Collateral Reviews

(1977), Standards Relating to Corrections Administration
(1977), Standards Relating to Court Organization and Ad-
ministration (1977), Standards Relating to Disposition (1977),
Standards Relating to Interim Status (1977), Standards Re-
lating to Police Handling of Juvenile Problems (1977),
Standards Relating to Pretrial Court Proceedings (1977),
Standards Relating to School and Education (1977), and
Standards Relating to Noncriminal Misbehavior (1977).

E. RESEARCH TECHNIQUES

Bibliographies and Bibliographical Guides

613. Harzfeld, Lois A. Periodical Indexes in the Social Sciences
and Humanities: A Subject Guide. Metuchen, N. J. :
Scarecrow, 1978. 174p.
The author has compiled an annotated guide to abstracts
and indexes in the humanities and social sciences. The
book has a comprehensive index and many cross-references.

614. Makar, Ragai N. A Selected List of Information Systems and
Services for Social Workers. Garden City, N. Y. :
Adelphi University Library, 1975. 115p.
Designed for social work researchers, this book provides
a classified listing of 127 libraries and information systems, with addresses, descriptions of services, scope of
subjects covered, holdings, and user restrictions. Subject
and information-system indexes are included.

615. Markle, Allan, and Roger C. Rinn, editors. Author's Guide
to Journals in Psychology, Psychiatry, and Social Work.
New York: Haworth, 1977. 256p.
This guide was designed for authors desiring to submit
manuscripts for consideration in the field of psychology,
psychiatry, and social work. The journals are arranged
alphabetically, with information on review period, acceptance ratio, manuscript preference areas, where the journal is indexed or abstracted, size of the journal's circulation, and other additional data about the journal itself.
There are three indexes: subject, title, and keyword.

616. Stang, David J. , and Lawrence S. Wrightsman. Dictionary of
Social Behavior and Social Research Methods. Monterey,
Calif. : Brooks/Cole, 1981. 105p.
This dictionary defines terms used in social psychology
and social research.

617. Sussman, Marvin B. Author's Guide to Journals in Sociology
and Related Fields. New York: Haworth, 1978. 214p.
Sussman supplies detailed information for publishing scholars

in the field of sociology and related areas, including social work. Other guides relevant to social work include
Author's Guide to Journals in the Health Field and Author's
Guide to Journals in Law, Criminal Justice and Criminology.

Handbook

618.   Struening, Elmer L., and Marcia Guttentag. Handbook of
          Evaluation Research. Beverly Hills, Calif.: Sage,
          1975, 2 vols.
        This publication provides a detailed survey of the evalua-
        tion of social action programs. Strategies and methods of
        evaluation are examined in the context of politics, social
        ecology, and human service programs, including mental
        health, public health, and compensatory education programs.
        Selective and cumulative bibliographies, numerous tables,
        and index are included.

Review

619.   Maas, Henry S., editor. Social Service Research: Review
          of Studies. Washington, D.C.: National Association of
          Social Workers, 1978. 232p.
        This work reviews and critically analyzes research done
        in the field of social service during the 1970s. The re-
        view is organized by population at risk: families, children
        in adoptive homes, children in foster families and institu-
        tions, troubled people and older people. Two other works
        have been published. The first volume is Five Fields of
        Social Service: Review of Research, which covers research
        completed through 1964. The second volume, Research in
        the Social Services: A Five Year Review, spans work done
        from 1965 to 1969.

Sourcebooks

620.   Reid, William J. "Mapping the Knowledge Base of Social
          Work." Social Work, 26 (March 1981), 124-132.
        Reid, professor at the School of Social Welfare, State Uni-
        versity of New York at Albany, discusses the classification
        of social work knowledge.

621.   Wakefield Washington Associates. Family Research: A Source
          Book, Analysis, and Guide to Federal Funding. West-
          port, Conn.: Greenwood, 1979. 945p. 2 vols.
        This guide provides basic information on federally funded
        and sponsored family research programs.

F. VITAL RECORDS

Index

622. Statistical Reference Index: A Selective Guide to American
Statistical Publications from Sources Other Than the
U.S. Government. Washington, D.C.: Congressional
Information Services, 1980- . Monthly, with annual
cumulation.
A supplement and complement to the Statistical Abstracts
of the United States (item 66), this publication provides
the most important index to statistics on social conditions,
government, politics, population, finance, and business
from selected U.S. sources other than the federal government.

Bibliographies

623. Gilmartin, Kevin J., and others. Social Indicators: An Annotated Bibliography on Current Literature. New York:
Garland, 1979. 123p.
This is a bibliography of current literature on social indicators, 1972-1978. Lengthy annotations accompany each
entry. There are two indexes: author and subject.

624. Wilcox, Leslie D. Social Indicators and Societal Monitoring.
San Francisco: Jossey-Bass, 1972. 464p.
Wilcox's book is a classified, annotated guide to over 600
books, articles, and documents dealing with social indicators and societal monitoring.

Directories

625. Birth ... Marriage ... Divorce ... Death--On the Record:
A Directory of 288 Primary Sources for Personal and
Family Records in the 50 States and Overseas Where
the U.S. Has Jurisdiction. Rye, N.Y.: Reymont,
1977. 46p.
This is a pocket-size directory to 288 official source records of family and personal records in the United States.
The listings give addresses, costs of record copying, and
dates at which records keeping began at each source.

626. Everton, George B., editor. The Handy Book for Genealogists.
Rev. and enl. ed. Logan, Utah: Everton, 1971. 298p.
Designed primarily for genealogists, this book would be
useful to social workers because it offers maps of all U.S.
counties, bibliographies of state and county histories, and
where to write for county records.

627. Where to Write for Birth and Death Records--U.S. and Out-

lying Areas.   Rockville, Md. : National Center for Health Statistics, Scientific and Technical Information Branch, 1976- . Irregular. DHEW Pub. No. 78-1142.

The National Center for Health Statistics periodically updates this pamphlet on where to write for information on death and birth records.

628.   Where to Write for Divorce Records--U.S. and Outlying Areas. Rockville, Md. : National Center for Health Statistics, Scientific and Technical Information Branch, 1976- . Irregular. DHEW Pub. No. 78-1145.

Similar to item 627, this directory gives the addresses of state and local offices where divorce records are located.   The National Center for Health Statistics periodically updates the publication.

629.   Where to Write for Marriage Records--U.S. and Outlying Areas. Rockville, Md. : National Center for Health Statistics, Scientific and Technical Information Branch, 1976- . Irregular. DHEW Pub. No. 78-1144.

This pamphlet tells where to write for local marriage records, lists cost of full copy and cost of short form, indicates any special requirements, and specifies dates of records held.

Social Indicators

630.   U.S. Bureau of the Census.   Social Indicators III: Selected Data on Social Conditions and Trends in the United States.   Washington, D.C. : Bureau of the Census. 1980.   584p.   S/N003-024-02683-0.

Social Indicators III continues the Social Indicators series. It gives comprehensive statistical data on the American family, social security and welfare benefits, social participation, housing problems, and other areas of interest to social workers.

631.   U.S. Office of Federal Statistical Policy and Standards.   Social Indicators, 1976: Selected Data on Social Conditions and Trends in the United States.   Washington, D.C. : Bureau of the Census, 1977.   564p.   S/N041-001-00156-5.

A source of comprehensive statistical data on social conditions in the U.S., this publication covers such areas as the family, housing, social security and welfare, health and nutrition, and social mobility and participation.   Each chapter has three main parts: the first part of each chapter contains an introductory text and charts; the second part has the statistical tables; and the third part provides technical notes.   There is a subject index.

632. U. S. Office of Federal Statistical Policy and Standards. Social Indicators, 1973: Selected Statistics on Social Conditions and Trends in the United States. Washington, D. C. : U. S. Government Printing Office, 1973. 258p. S/N0324-00256.

Social Indicators, the result of four years of research, provides a wealth of statistical data on eight broad areas of concern to social workers: health, public safety, education, employment, income, housing, leisure and recreation, and population. Some 165 charts and tables give an indicated measure of individual and family well-being in the U. S. National totals are broken down by age, sex, and racial characteristics, and sources of statistical data are noted at the bottom of each table. All statistics are footnoted.

Statistics

633. Vital Statistics of the United States. Washington, D. C. : National Center for Health Statistics, 1940- . Annual. C3-139:937/1-2.

Vital Statistics is a basic source for birth, mortality, marriage, and divorce statistics for the United States and its possessions.

6. SOCIAL WORK PROFESSION

A. SOCIAL WORK PRACTICE

Directory

634. NASW Register of Clinical Social Workers. Washington, D. C.:
     National Association of Social Workers, 1976- . Ir-
     regular.
     The register lists almost 8,000 state-licensed and Academy
     of Certified Social Workers (ACSW) practitioners. All
     listings have been reviewed by professional peers and give
     credentials and specialization areas of practitioners. Also
     included are a definition of clinical social work and a glos-
     sary of terms. The Association published a supplement in
     1978, which updated the main volume with 2,600 new names.

Handbook

635. Handbook on the Private Practice of Social Work. Rev. ed.
     Washington, D. C.: National Association of Social Work-
     ers, 1974. 63p.
     This handbook provides a broad overview of private and
     social casework.

Manual

636. Manual for Adjudication of Grievances. Washington, D. C.:
     National Association of Social Workers, 1973. 120p.
     This four-part manual offers policies and procedures adopted
     by the Delegate Assembly of NASW. Policy and Proce-
     dures for Chapters in Handling Grievances is reprinted in
     the appendix.

Standards

637. NASW Standards for Social Work Personnel Practices. New
     York: National Association of Social Workers, 1971.
     31p.
     The National Association of Social Workers has also published
     a Code of Ethics.

B. SOCIAL WORK EDUCATION

Indexes

638. Current Index to Journals in Education (CIJE). Phoenix:
        Oryx, 1969- . Monthly, with annual cumulation.
        Complements and supplements Resources in Education (item
        639) and Education Index. CIJE is a selective index to ed-
        ucational materials in over 700 journals. Separate sub-
        ject and author indexes refer users to the annotated main
        entry section. CIJE is available online.

639. Resources in Education (RIE). Washington, D. C. : Educational
        Resources Information Center, 1966- . Monthly, with
        annual cumulation. Published by Oryx Press.
        Published monthly with annual cumulations, RIE is the
        companion volume to CIJE in the ERIC system. RIE in-
        dexes books, documents, reports, proceedings, papers,
        and curriculum material by subject, author, and sponsor-
        ing institution. Abstracts are provided for all the articles
        listed and approximately 80% of the articles are available
        on microfiche. RIE can be computer-searched. Subject
        areas covered pertinent to social work include educating
        the handicapped, mental health and mental retardation, so-
        cial services in the schools, and social work education.

Bibliographies

640. Elwell, Mary Ellen, compiler. Films for Use in Teaching
        Social Welfare and Where to Find Them. Atlanta: Fa-
        culty Development for Undergraduate Social Welfare Ed-
        ucation Project, Southern Regional Educational Board,
        1971. 49p.
        A guide to 250 16mm films, this publication supplies in-
        formation on whether the film is in black-and-white or
        color, running time, date of production, content, and at
        least one source for obtaining the film.

641. Li, Hong-Chan. Social Work Education: A Bibliography.
        Metuchen, N. J. : Scarecrow, 1978. 341p.
        This is a comprehensive bibliography of over 3,300 books,
        periodical articles, proceedings, reports, documents, pam-
        phlets, and dissertations published between 1960 and 1976
        on postsecondary social work education. The bibliography
        is not annotated. The entries are arranged by subject
        matter in 17 chapters.

642. Loavenbruck, Grant, and Carol Crecca. Continuing Social
        Work Education: An Annotated Bibliography. New York:
        Council on Social Work Education, 1980. 113p.
        Some 144 citations from four subject areas--social work,
        continuing education, mental health, and adult education/

learning theory--are included in this annotated bibliography.
The bulk of the publications selected appeared during the
1970s.   The entries are arranged into four sections: Continuing Education: Overviews about CE Practice and Phi-
losophies; Theoretical Underpinnings; Continuing Education
Methodologies; and Continuing Education Policies and Related Regulations.

643.   Matson, Margaret B., and Sheldon R. Gelman, editors. Building the Undergraduate Social Work Library: An Annotated Bibliography. New York: Council on Social Work
Education, 1980. 77p.
The compilers have collected a comprehensive bibliography
of materials necessary for a complete collection of major
sources for the undergraduate social work library.

644.   Morris, Clare.   Literature and the Social Worker: A Reading
List for Practitioners, Teachers, Students and Voluntary
Workers. London: Library Association, 1975. 283p.
Published by the British Library Association, this annotated
bibliography cites works of fiction that illustrate problems
of professional interest to social workers.   Entries are
arranged by subject.

645.   Yao, Winberta M., compiler.   United States Government Publications in Social Welfare: A Selected Bibliography.
2nd ed. New York: Council on Social Work Education,
1956. 81p.
This retrospective bibliography lists U.S. government publications in the field of social welfare.

Directories

646.   Gartner, Alan, editor.   College Programs for Paraprofessionals: A Directory of Degree-Granting Programs in the
Human Services. New York: Human Sciences, 1975.
112p.
The book identifies 950 degree-granting programs in the
human services for paraprofessionals.   Arranged alphabetically by state, the directory gives information on the name
of the college, address, telephone number, person respon-
sible for the program, department name, and in some
cases the type of program offered.

647.   Schools of Social Work Offering Doctoral Programs and Third-
Year Post-Master's Programs. New York: Council on
Social Work Education, 1980. 5p.
This directory lists colleges and universities offering post-
master's and doctoral programs in social work.   The CSWE
does not accredit these programs.   The publication is regu-
larly updated by the Council.

648. Schools of Social Work with Accredited Master's Degree Programs. New York: Council on Social Work Education, 1980. 15p.
The Council has compiled a list of colleges and universities with CSWE-accredited graduate degree programs in social work. Entries give the school name, address, dean or director, telephone number, year it first received accreditation, and year of the next review. Also included are Canadian schools of social work and schools in candidacy status. The list is periodically updated.

649. Stickney, Patricia, and Rose Perla Resnick, compilers. World Guide to Social Work Education. New York: International Association of Schools of Social Work, 1974. 297p.
Although somewhat dated, this directory is a selective, not comprehensive, survey of 79 representative schools of social work in 65 countries. It provides information about the history of each school, its objectives, its requirements, the duration of training, and the curriculum. In addition, it includes a description of 22 national and regional associations of schools of social work and the International Association of Schools of Social Work.

650. Summary Information of Master of Social Work Programs. New York: Council on Social Work Education, 197?- . Annual.
This CSWE directory summarizes information about CSWE-accredited graduate schools and graduate schools working toward accreditation. Listed are degrees offered, the number of applications, filing dates, tuition and related fees, concentrations offered, practicum arrangements, advanced standing information and part-time study provisions, usual time span for enrollment to graduation, and whether the school offers a doctorate in social work. Information on schools offering a baccalaureate in social work may be found in the CSWE's Colleges and Universities Summary, published in 1976.

Handbooks

651. Baer, Betty L., and Ronald C. Federico, eds. Educating the Baccalaureate Social Worker: Report of the Undergraduate Social Work Curriculum Development Project. Cambridge, Mass.: Ballinger, 1978. 238p.
Baer and Federico examine the content, method, and structure of the baccalaureate social work curriculum. The volume has three appendixes: Position Papers on Issues of Significance to Social Work Education; Knowledge, Values, and Skill Essential for the Attainment of the Entry Level Compentencies; and List of Resource Persons to the Project. See also item 652.

652.   Educating the Baccalaureate Social Worker: A Curriculum De-
       velopment Resource Guide. Vol. 2. Edited by Betty
       L. Baer and Ronald C. Federico. Cambridge, Mass.:
       Ballinger, 1979. 261p.
       A companion volume to item 651, this book consists of a
       series of papers on structure and curriculum of under-
       graduate social work programs.

Manual

653.   Rosenberg, Janet. Breakfast: Two Jars of Paste: A Train-
       ing Manual for Workers in the Human Services. Cleve-
       land: Press of Case Western Reserve University, 1972.
       125p.
       The author designed this manual for training paraprofes-
       sionals and baccalaureate-level professionals in the basics
       of social service. Curriculum materials, which include
       games and exercises as well as case histories and useful
       readings, are included in the text.

Standards

654.   Manual of Accrediting Standards for Professional Schools of
       Social Work. New York: Council on Social Work Edu-
       cation, 1971. 79p.
       Chapter 1 is a general statement of standards for accre-
       diting schools of social work by the National Commission
       on Accrediting. The succeeding chapters contain the Com-
       mission's interpretation and elaboration of the general stand-
       ards. Standards for master's programs and standards for
       post-master's programs are found in Appendix VI.

655.   Standards for the Accreditation of Baccalaureate Degree Pro-
       grams in Social Work. New York: Council on Social
       Work Education, 1974.
       The Council on Social Work Education outlines the essential
       elements of a baccalaureate degree program in social work.

Statistics

656.   Statistics on Social Work Education in the United States. New
       York: Council on Social Work Education, 1972- . An-
       nual.
       Enrollment statistics for CSWE-accredited social work
       schools are presented in this publication, which contains
       information on student and faculty characteristics, degrees
       awarded, programs offered, etc. The 1981 edition has
       school-by-school breakdowns on baccalaureate and doctoral
       programs.

A. SOCIAL WORK JOURNALS

Administration

Administration in Mental Health. National Institute of Mental Health, P. O. Box 2088, Rockville, MD 20852. 1972- . Semiannual.

Administration in Social Work. Haworth Press, 149 Fifth Ave., New York, NY 10010. 1977- . Quarterly.

Administrative Science Quarterly. Cornell University, Graduate School of Business and Public Administration, Ithaca, NY 14853. 1956- . Quarterly.

Advanced Management Journal. Society for Advancement of Management, 135 W. 50th St., New York, NY 10020. 1935- . Quarterly.

The Bureaucrat. American Society for Public Instruction, National Capital Area Chapter, 1225 Connecticut Ave., N.W., Washington, DC 20036. 1972- . Quarterly.

Compensation Review. American Management Associations, AMACOM Division, 135 W. 50th St., New York, NY 10020. 1969- . Quarterly.

Hospital Health Services Administration. American College of Hospital Administrators, 840 N. Lake Shore Dr., Chicago, IL 60611. 1956- . Quarterly.

Inquiry: A Journal of Medical Care Organization, Provision and Financing. Blue Cross Association, 840 N. Lake Shore Dr., Chicago, IL 60611. 1963- . Quarterly.

Journal for Medicaid Management. U. S. Health Care Financing Administration, Medicaid Bureau, Room 4628, Mary E. Switzer Building, 330 C St., S.W., Washington, DC 20201. 1977- . Quarterly.

Journal of Mental Health Administration. Association of Mental Health Administrators, Suite 3, 4131 N. Grand River, Lansing, MI 48906. 1972- . Quarterly.

Journal of Systems Management. Association for Systems Management, 24587 Bagley Rd., Cleveland, OH 44138. 1948- . Monthly.

Management Review. American Management Associations, 135 W. 50th St., New York, NY 10020. 1923- . Monthly.

New Directions for Program Evaluation. Jossey-Bass, 433 California St., San Francisco, CA 94104. 1978- . Quarterly.

Personnel. American Management Associations, AMACOM Division, 135 W. 50th St., New York, NY 10020. 1919- . Bimonthly.

Public Administration Review. American Society for Public Administration, 1225 Connecticut Ave., N.W., Washington, DC 20036. 1940- . Quarterly.

Supervisory Management. American Management Associations, AMACOM Division, 135 W. 50th St., New York, NY 10020. 1955- . Monthly.

Aging and the Aged

Aged Care and Counseling. Haworth Press, 149 Fifth Ave., New York, NY 10010. 1977- . Bimonthly.

Aged Care & Services Review. Haworth Press, 149 Fifth Ave., New York, NY 10010. 1977- . Bimonthly.

Aging. U.S. Department of Health and Human Resources, Administration on Aging, 400 Sixth St., S.W., Washington, DC 20201. 1951- . Ten issues per year.

Educational Gerontology. Hemisphere Publishing, 1025 Vermont Ave. N.W., Washington, DC 20005. 1976- . Quarterly.

Gerontologist. Gerontological Society, 1835 K St., N.W., Washington, DC 20006. 1961- . Bimonthly.

International Journal of Aging and Human Development. Baywood Publishing, 120 Marine St., Farmingdale, NY 11735. 1973- . Quarterly.

Journal of Geriatric Psychiatry. International Universities Press, 239 Park Ave. S., New York, NY 10003. 1967- . Semiannual.

Journal of Gerontological Social Work. Haworth Press, 149 Fifth Ave., New York, NY 10010. 1978- . Quarterly.

Journal of Gerontology. Gerontological Society, Suite 520, One Dupont Circle, Washington, DC 20036. 1946- . Quarterly.

Journal of the American Geriatrics Society. American Geriatrics

Society, 10 Columbus Circle, New York, NY 10019. 1953- .
Monthly.

Child and Youth Welfare

Adolescence. Libra Publishers, 391 Willets Rd., Roslyn Heights,
NY 11577. 1966- . Quarterly.

Caring. National Committee for the Prevention of Child Abuse, 111
E. Wacker Dr., Chicago, IL 60601. 1975. Quarterly.

Child Abuse & Neglect. Pergamon Press, Maxwell House, Fairview
Park, Elmsford, NY 10523. 1977- . Quarterly.

Child & Youth Services. Haworth Press, 149 Fifth Ave., New York,
NY 10010. 1977- . Bimonthly.

Child Care Quarterly. Human Sciences Press, 72 Fifth Ave., New
York, NY 10011. 1971- . Quarterly.

Child Development. University of Chicago Press, 5801 S. Ellis Ave.,
Chicago, IL 60637. 1930- . Quarterly.

Child Psychiatry and Human Development. Human Sciences Press,
72 Fifth Ave., New York, NY 10011. 1970- . Quarterly.

Child Study Journal. State University of New York, 1300 Elmwood
Ave., Buffalo, NY 14222. 1970- . Quarterly.

Child Welfare. Child Welfare League of America, 67 Irving Place,
New York, NY 10003. 1920- . Ten issues per year.

Children and Youth Services Review. Pergamon Press, Maxwell
House, Fairview Park, Elmsford, NY 10523. 1979- . Quarterly.

Children Today. U.S. Office of Child Development, P.O. Box 1182,
Washington, DC 20013. 1972- . Bimonthly.

Day Care and Early Education: The Magazine of the Child-growth
Movement. Human Sciences Press, 72 Fifth Ave., New York,
NY 10011. 1973- . Quarterly.

Exceptional Children. Council for Exceptional Children, 1920 Association Dr., Reston, VA 22091. 1934- . Eight issues per
year.

International Child Welfare Review. International Union for Child
Welfare, P.O. Box 41, 1211 Geneva 20, Switzerland. 1926- .
Quarterly.

Journal of Experimental Child Psychology. Academic Press, 111
Fifth Ave., New York, NY 10003. 1964- . Eight issues per
year.

Journal of Pediatrics. C. V. Mosby, 11830 Westline Industrial Dr.,
St. Louis, MO 63141. 1932- . Monthly.

Journal of the American Academy of Child Psychiatry. American
Academy of Child Psychiatry, 92A Yale Sta., New Haven, CT
06520. 1962- . Quarterly.

Journal of Youth and Adolescence. Plenum Publishing, 227 W. 17th
St., New York, NY 10011. 1972- . Bimonthly.

Maternal-Child Nursing Journal. University of Pittsburgh, Pediatric
and Obstetrical Nursing Dept., 437 Victoria Bldg., 3500 Victoria
St., Pittsburgh, PA 15213. 1972- . Quarterly.

Pediatrics. American Academy of Pediatrics, P.O. Box 1034,
Evanston, IL 60204. 1948- . Monthly.

Washington Report on Children's Services. Child Welfare League of
America, 1346 Connecticut Ave., N.W., Washington, DC 20036.
1976- . Monthly.

Youth and Society. Sage Publications, 275 S. Beverly Dr., Beverly
Hills, CA 90212. 1969- . Quarterly.

Crime and Delinquency

Crime and Delinquency. National Council on Crime and Delinquency,
411 Hackensack Ave., Hackensack, NJ 07601. 1955- . Quarterly.

Crime & Social Justice. Issues in Criminology, P.O. Box 4373,
Berkeley, CA 94704. 1974- . Semiannual.

Criminal Justice and Behavior. Sage Publications, 275 S. Beverly
Dr., Beverly Hills, CA 90212. 1974- . Quarterly.

Criminology: An Interdisciplinary Journal. Sage Publications, 275
S. Beverly Dr., Beverly Hills, CA 90212. 1963- . Quarterly.

Federal Probation: A Journal of Correctional Philosophy and Practice. U.S. Administrative Office of the United States Courts,
Supreme Court Building, Washington, DC 20544. 1936- . Quarterly.

International Journal of Offender Therapy and Comparative Criminology. Association for Psychiatric Treatment of Offenders, 199
Gloucester Place, London NW1 6BU, England. 1957- . Three
issues per year.

Journal of Criminal Law & Criminology. Williams & Wilkins, 428
E. Preston St., Baltimore, MD 21202. 1910- . Quarterly.

Journal of Offender Counseling Services and Rehabilitation. Haworth

Press, 149 Fifth Ave., New York, NY 10010. 1976- . Quarterly. (Formerly Offender Rehabilitation.)

Journal of Research in Crime and Delinquency. National Council on Crime and Delinquency, 411 Hackensack Ave., Hackensack, NJ 07601. 1964- . Semiannual.

Law and Behavior. Research Press, 2612 N. Mattis Ave., Champaign, IL 61820. 1976- . Quarterly.

Drug and Alcohol Abuse

Addiction and Substance Abuse Report. Grafton Publications, 667 Madison Ave., New York, NY 10021. 1970- . Monthly. (Formerly Addiction and Drug Abuse Report.)

Contemporary Drug Problems. Federal Legal Publications, 157 Chambers St., New York, NY 10007. 1971/72- . Quarterly.

Drug Abuse & Alcoholism Review. Haworth Press, 149 Fifth Ave., New York, NY 10010. 1978- . Bimonthly.

Drug Forum--The Journal of Human Issues. Baywood Publishing, 43 Central Dr., Farmingdale, NY 11735. 1971- . Quarterly.

International Journal of the Addictions. Marcel Dekker, 270 Madison Ave., New York, NY 10016. 1966- . Eight issues per year.

Journal of Drug Issues. Rachin, P.O. Box 4021, Tallahassee, FL 32303. 1971- . Quarterly.

Journal of Studies on Alcohol. Rutgers Center of Alcohol Studies, New Brunswick, NJ 08903. 1940- . Quarterly.

Economics

American Economic Review. American Economic Association, Suite 812, Oxford House, 1313 21st Ave. S., Nashville, TN 37212. 1911- . Quarterly.

American Journal of Economics and Sociology. American Journal of Economics and Sociology, 50 E. 69th St., New York, NY 10021. 1911- . Quarterly.

Harvard Business Review. Harvard University, Graduate School of Business Administration, Soldiers Field, Boston, MA 02163. 1922- . Bimonthly.

International Labour Review. Bureau International du Travail, CH 1211 Geneva 22, Switzerland. 1921- . Bimonthly.

Quarterly Journal of Economics. John Wiley and Sons, 605 Third
Ave., New York, NY 10016. 1886- . Eight issues per year.

Review of Black Political Economy. Transaction Periodicals Consortium, Rutgers University, New Brunswick, NJ 08903. 1970- .
Quarterly.

Education

Academic Therapy. Academic Therapy Publications, 20 Commercial
Blvd., Novato, CA 94947. 1965- . Five issues per year.

Black Scholar. Black World Foundation, Box 908, Sausalito, CA
94965. 1969- . Ten issues per year.

The Canadian Journal of Social Work Education/Revue Canadienne
d' Education en Servie Social. Canadian Association of Schools
of Social Work, Suite 909, 151 Slater St., Ottawa, Ontario KIP5H3,
Canada. 1974- . Three issues per year.

Child Study Journal. State University of New York, 1300 Elmwood
Ave., Buffalo, NY 14222. 1970- . Quarterly.

Day Care and Early Education: The Magazine of the Child-growth
Movement. Human Sciences Press, 72 Fifth Ave., New York,
NY 10011. 1973- . Quarterly.

Death Education: Pedagogy-Counseling-Care, an International Quarterly. Hemisphere Publishing, 1025 Vermont Ave., N.W., Washington, DC 20005. 1977- . Quarterly.

Education and Training of the Mentally Retarded. Council for Exceptional Children, 1920 Association Dr., Reston, VA 22091.
1966- . Quarterly.

Educational Gerontology. Hemisphere Publishing, 1025 Vermont
Ave., N.W., Washington, DC 20005. 1976- . Quarterly.

Elementary School Guidance & Counseling. American Personnel and
Guidance Association, Two Skyline Place, Suite 400, 5203 Leesburg Pike, Falls Church, VA 22041. 1967- . Quarterly.

Harvard Educational Review. Harvard University, Graduate School
of Education, Longfellow Hall 13, Appian Way, Cambridge, MA
02138. 1931- . Quarterly.

Journal of Education for Social Work. Council of Social Work Education, 111 Eighth Ave., New York, NY 10011. 1965- . Three
issues per year.

Journal of Extension. Extension Journal, 605 Extension Building,
432 N. Lake St., Madison, WI 53706. 1963- . Bimonthly.

Journal of Negro Education. Howard University, Bureau of Educational Research, 20040 Sixth St., N.W., Washington, DC 20059. 1932- . Quarterly.

Journal of School Health. American School Health Association, P.O. Box 708, Kent, OH 44240. 1931- . Monthly, except July and August.

Journal of School Psychology. Human Sciences Press, 72 Fifth Ave., New York, NY 10011. 1963- . Quarterly.

School Counselor. American Personnel and Guidance Association, Two Skyline Place, Suite 400, 5203 Leesburg Pike, Falls Church, VA 22041. 1952- . Five issues per year.

School Social Work Journal. Illinois Association of School Social Workers, Northlake, IL 60164. 1977- . Semiannual.

School Social Work Quarterly. Haworth Press, 149 Fifth Ave., New York, NY 10010. 1979- . Quarterly.

Social Work Education Reporter. Council on Social Work Education, 111 Eighth Ave., New York, NY 10011. 1953- . Three issues per year.

Social Work in Education: A Journal of School Social Work. National Association of Social Workers, Two Park Ave., New York, NY 10016. 1978- . Quarterly.

Family Life

American Journal of Family Therapy. Brunner Mazel, 19 Union Sq. W., New York, NY 10003. 1973- . Quarterly.

Family Coordinator: Journal of Education, Council on Family Relations. 1219 University Ave., S.E., Minneapolis, MN 55414. 1952- . Quarterly.

Family Life. American Institute of Family Relations, 5287 Sunset Blvd., Los Angeles, CA 90027. 1941- . Bimonthly.

Family Planning Perspectives. Alan Guttmacher Institute, 515 Madison Ave., New York, NY 10022. 1969- . Bimonthly.

Family Process: A Multidisciplinary Journal of Family Study, Research & Treatment. Family Process, 149 E. 78th St., New York, NY 10021. 1962- . Quarterly.

Family Service Highlights. Family Service Association of America, 44 E. 23rd St., New York, NY 10010. 1940- . Bimonthly.

Family Therapy. Libra Publishers, 391 Willets Rd., Roslyn Heights, NY 11577. 1974- . Three issues per year.

International Family Planning Perspectives and Digest. Alan Guttmacher Institute, 515 Madison Ave., New York, NY 10022.
1975- . Quarterly.

International Journal of Family Counseling. Transaction Periodicals
Consortium, Rutgers University, New Brunswick, NJ 08903.
1973- . Semiannual. (Formerly The Journal of Family Counseling.)

International Journal of Family Therapy. Human Sciences Press,
72 Fifth Ave., New York, NY 10011. 1979- . Quarterly.

Journal of Comparative Family Studies. University of Calgary, Department of Sociology, 2920 24th Ave., N.W., Calgary, Alberta,
Canada. 1970- . Three issues per year.

Journal of Divorce. Haworth Press, 149 Fifth Ave., New York,
NY 10010. 1977- . Quarterly.

Journal of Family History. The National Council on Family Relations, 1219 University Ave., S.E., Minneapolis, MN 55414.
1976- . Quarterly. (Succeeds Family in Historical Perspective.)

Journal of Family Law. University of Louisville, School of Law,
Louisville, KY 40208. 1961- . Quarterly.

Journal of Family Practice. Appleton-Century-Crofts, 292 Madison
Ave., New York, NY 10017. 1974- . Monthly.

Journal of Marital and Family Therapy. American Association for
Marriage and Family Therapy, 924 W. Ninth, Upland, CA 91786.
1975- . Quarterly.

Journal of Marriage and the Family. National Council on Family
Relations, 1219 University Ave., S.E., Minneapolis, MN 55414.
1938- . Quarterly.

Journal of Sex and Marital Therapy. Human Sciences Press, 72
Fifth Ave., New York, NY 10011. 1975- . Quarterly.

Marriage & Family Review. Haworth Press, 149 Fifth Ave., New
York, NY 10010. 1977- . Bimonthly.

Single Parent. Parents Without Partners, 7910 Woodmont Ave.,
Washington, DC 20014. 1958- . Monthly.

Studies in Family Planning. Population Council, One Dag Hammer-
skjold Plaza, New York, NY 10017. 1963- . Monthly.

Health Care

American Journal of Nursing. American Nursing Association, 10
Columbus Circle, NY 10019. 1900- . Monthly.

American Journal of Public Health. American Public Health Association, 1015 18th St., N.W., Washington, DC 20036. 1911- . Monthly.

Health Services Research. Hospital Research and Educational Trust, 840 N. Lake Shore Dr., Chicago, IL 60611. 1966- . Quarterly.

Hospital & Community Psychiatry. American Psychiatric Association, 1700 18th St., N.W., Washington, DC 20009. 1950- . Monthly.

Hospital and Health Services Administration. American College of Hospital Administrators, 840 N. Lake Shore Dr., Chicago, IL 60611. 1956- . Quarterly.

Hospital Progress. Catholic Hospital Association, 143 S. Grand Blvd., St. Louis, MO 63104. 1920- . Monthly.

Hospitals. American Hospital Association, 840 N. Lake Shore Dr., Chicago, IL 60611. 1936- . Semiannual.

Inquiry: A Journal of Medical Care Organization, Provision and Financing. Blue Cross Association, 840 N. Lake Shore Dr., Chicago, IL 60611. 1963- . Quarterly.

JAMA: The Journal of the American Medical Association. American Medical Association, 535 N. Dearborn St., Chicago, IL 60610. 1848- . Weekly.

Journal of Chronic Diseases. Pergamon Press, Headington Hill Hall, Oxford OX3 OBW, England. 1955- . Monthly.

Journal of Medicaid Management. U. S. Health Care Financing Administration, Medicaid Bureau, Mary E. Switzer Building, Room 4628, 330 C St., S.W., Washington, DC 20201. 1977- . Quarterly.

Journal of Psychiatric Nursing and Mental Health Services. Charles B. Slack, 6900 Grove Rd., Thorofare, NJ 08086. 1963- . Monthly.

Journal of School Health. American School Health Association, P.O. Box 708, Kent, OH 44240. 1931- . Monthly, except July and August.

Maternal-Child Nursing Journal. University of Pittsburgh, Pediatric and Obstetrical Nursing Dept., 437 Victoria Building, 3500 Victoria St., Pittsburgh, PA 15213. 1972- . Quarterly.

New England Journal of Medicine. Massachusetts Medical Society, 10 Shattuck St., Boston, MA 02115. 1901- . Monthly.

Nursing Outlook. American Journal of Nursing, 10 Columbus Circle, New York, NY 10019. 1953- . Monthly.

Nursing Research. American Journal of Nursing, 10 Columbus Circle, New York, NY 10019. 1952- . Bimonthly.

Pediatrics. American Academy of Pediatrics, P.O. Box 1034, Evanston, IL 60204. 1948- . Monthly.

Psychosomatic Medicine. Elsevier Publishing, 52 Vanderbilt Ave., New York, NY 10017. 1938- . Eight issues per year.

Social Work in Health Care. Haworth Press, 149 Fifth Ave., New York, NY 10010. 1975- . Quarterly.

Mental Health

Administration in Mental Health. Human Sciences Press, 72 Fifth Ave., New York, NY 10011. 1972- . Semiannual.

Community Mental Health Journal. Human Sciences Press, 72 Fifth Ave., New York, NY 10011. 1965- . Quarterly.

Community Mental Health Review. Haworth Press, 149 Fifth Ave., New York, NY 10010. 1975- . Bimonthly.

Family and Child Mental Health. Human Sciences Press, 72 Fifth Ave., New York, NY 10011. 1974- . Semiannually.

Journal of Mental Health Administration. Association of Mental Health Administration, 4131 N. Grand River, Lansing, MI 48906. 1972- . Quarterly.

Politics

American Political Science Review. American Political Science Association, 1527 New Hampshire Ave., N.W., Washington, DC 20036. 1906- . Quarterly.

Commentary: Journal of Significant Thought and Opinion on Contemporary Issues. American Jewish Committee, 165 E. 56th St., New York, NY 10027. 1945- . Monthly.

Political Science Quarterly. Academy of Political Science, Suite 500, 114th St., New York, NY 10025. 1886- . Quarterly.

Psychiatry

American Journal of Psychiatry. American Psychiatric Association, 1700 18th St., N.W., Washington, DC 20009. 1844- . Monthly.

Archives of General Psychiatry. American Medical Association, 535 N. Dearborn St., Chicago, IL 60610. 1959- . Monthly.

Child Psychiatry & Human Development. Human Sciences Press, 72 Fifth Ave., New York, NY 10011. 1970- . Quarterly.

Comprehensive Psychiatry. Grune & Stratton, 111 Fifth Ave., New York, NY 10017. 1960- . Bimonthly.

Hospital & Community Psychiatry. American Psychiatric Association, 1700 18th St., N.W., Washington, DC 20009. 1950- . Monthly.

International Journal of Psychiatry in Medicine. Baywood Publishing, 120 Marine St., Farmingdale, NY 11735. 1970- . Quarterly.

International Journal of Social Psychiatry. Avenue Publishing, 18 Park Ave., London NW11 7SJ, England. 1955- . Quarterly.

Journal of Nervous and Mental Disease. Williams & Wilkins, 428 East Preston St., Baltimore, MD 21202. 1874- . Monthly.

Journal of Psychiatric Nursing and Mental Health Services. Charles B. Slack, 6900 Grove Rd., Thorofare, NJ 08086. 1963- . Monthly.

Journal of the American Academy of Child Psychiatry. American Academy of Child Psychiatry, 92A Yale Sta., New Haven, CT 06520. 1961- . Quarterly.

Psychiatric Quarterly. Human Sciences Press, 72 Fifth Ave., New York, NY 10011.

Psychiatry: Journal for the Study of Interpersonal Processes. William Alanson White Psychiatric Foundation, 1610 New Hampshire Ave., N.W., Washington, DC 20009. 1938- . Quarterly.

Psychology

American Behavioral Scientist. Sage Publications, 275 S. Beverly Dr., Beverly Hills, CA 90202. 1957- . Bimonthly.

American Journal of Psychoanalysis. Association for the Advancement of Psychoanalysis, 329 E. 62nd St., New York, NY 10021. 1941- . Quarterly.

American Journal of Psychology. University of Illinois Press, 53 E. Gregory, P.O. Box 5081, Sta. A, Champaign, IL 61820. 1887- . Quarterly.

American Journal of Psychotherapy. Association for the Advancement of Psychotherapy, 114 E. 78th St., New York, NY 10021. 1946- . Quarterly.

American Psychologist. American Psychological Association, 1200 17th St., N.W., Washington, DC 20036. 1946- . Monthly.

Behavior Modification. Sage Publications, 275 S. Beverly Dr.,
Beverly Hills, CA 90212. 1977- . Quarterly.

Behavior Research and Therapy: An International Multidisciplinary
Journal. Pergamon Press, Maxwell House, Fairview Park, Elmsford, NY 10523. 1963- . Bimonthly.

Behavior Therapy. Academic Press, 111 Fifth Ave., New York,
NY 10003. 1970- . Five issues per year.

Behavioral Science. Society for General Systems Research, P.O.
Box 1055, Louisville, KY 40201. 1956- . Bimonthly.

Contemporary Psychoanalysis. William Alanson White Psychoanalytic Institute, 20 W. 74th St., New York, NY 10023. 1964- .
Quarterly.

Group & Organization Studies. University Associates Publishers,
7569 Eads Ave., La Jolla, CA 92037. 1976- . Quarterly.

Group Psychotherapy, Psychodrama and Sociometry. Beacon House,
P.O. Box 311, Beacon, NY 12503. 1947- . Quarterly.

International Journal of Group Psychotherapy. International Universities Press, 315 Fifth Ave., New York, NY 10016. 1951- .
Quarterly.

Journal of Abnormal Psychology. American Psychological Association, 1200 17th St., N.W., Washington, DC 20036. 1965- .
Bimonthly.

Journal of Applied Behavioral Science. NTL Institute for Applied
Behavioral Science, P.O. Box 9155, Rosslyn Sta., Arlington, VA
22209. 1965- . Quarterly.

Journal of Clinical Psychology. Clinical Psychology Publishing, 4
Conant Sq., Brandon, VT 05733. 1945- . Quarterly.

Journal of Contemporary Psychotherapy. Human Sciences Press,
72 Fifth Ave., New York, NY 10011. 1968- . Semiannual.

Journal of Counseling Psychology. American Psychological Association, 1200 17th St., N.W., Washington, DC 20036. 1954- .
Bimonthly.

Journal of Experimental Child Psychology. Academic Press, 111
Fifth Ave., New York, NY 10003. 1964- . Eight issues per
year.

Journal of General Psychology. Journal Press, 2 Commercial St.,
Provincetown, MA 02657. 1927- . Quarterly.

Journal of Genetic Psychology. Journal Press, 2 Commercial St.,
Provincetown, MA 02657. 1891- . Quarterly.

Journal of Personality. Duke University Press, P. O. Box 6697, College Sta., Durham, NC 27708. 1932- . Quarterly.

Journal of Personality and Social Psychology. American Psychological Association, 1200 17th St., N.W., Washington, DC 20036. 1965- . Monthly.

Journal of Psychology. Journal Press, 2 Commerical St., Provincetown, MA 02657. 1935/36- . Quarterly.

Journal of Social Psychology. Journal Press, 2 Commercial St., Provincetown, MA 02657. 1930- . Bimonthly.

Journal of the American Academy of Psychoanalysis. John Wiley and Sons, 605 Third Ave., New York, NY 10016. Quarterly.

Journal of the American Psychoanalytic Association. International University Press, 315 Fifth Ave., New York, NY 10016. 1953- . Quarterly.

Merrill-Palmer Quarterly of Behavior and Development. Merrill-Palmer Institute, 71 E. Ferry Ave., Detroit, MI 48202. 1954- . Quarterly.

Omega-Journal of Death & Dying. Greenwood Periodicals, 120 Marine St., Farmingdale, NY 11735. 1970- . Quarterly.

Pastoral Psychology. Human Sciences Press, 72 Fifth Ave., New York, NY 10011. 1950- . Monthly.

Personnel and Guidance Journal. American Personnel and Guidance Association, Two Skyline Place, 5203 Leesburg Pike, Falls Church, VA 22041. 1922- . Monthly, except July and August.

Psychoanalytic Quarterly. Psychoanalytic Quarterly, 57 W. 57th St., New York, NY 10019. 1932- . Quarterly.

Psychoanalytic Review: An American Journal of Psychoanalytic Psychology Devoted to the Understanding of Behavior and Culture. Human Sciences Press, 72 Fifth Ave., New York, NY 10011. 1913- . Quarterly.

Psychological Bulletin. American Psychological Association, 1200 17th St., N.W., Washington, DC 20036. 1904- . Bimonthly.

Psychological Review. American Psychological Association, 1200 17th St., N.W., Washington, DC 20036. 1925- . Bimonthly.

Psychology Today. Ziff Davis Publishing, One Park Ave., New York, NY 10016. 1967- . Monthly.

Psychotherapy: Theory, Research and Practice. University of Chicago, Dept. of Psychology, 5848 University Ave., Chicago, IL 60637. 1963- . Quarterly.

Social Psychology Quarterly. American Sociological Association, 17722 N St., N.W., Washington, DC 20036. 1937- . Quarterly.

Suicide and Life-Threatening Behavior. Human Sciences Press, 72 Fifth Ave., New York, NY 10011. 1970- . Quarterly.

Vocational Guidance Quarterly. National Vocational Guidance Association, 1607 New Hampshire Ave., N.W., Washington, DC 20009. 1952- . Quarterly.

Rehabilitation

American Journal of Occupational Therapy. American Occupational Therapy Association, 6000 Executive Blvd., Rockville, MD 20852. 1947- . Ten issues per year.

American Rehabilitation. U.S. Rehabilitation Services Administration, Mary E. Switzer Building, Room 1424, 330 C St., S.W., Washington, DC 20201. 1975- . Bimonthly.

Blindness. American Association of Workers for the Blind, 1511 K St., Washington, DC 20005. 1964- . Annual.

The Exceptional Parent: Children with Disabilities/Practical Guidance. Psy-Ed Corp., Room 700, Statler Office Building, 20 Providence St., Boston, MA 02116. 1971- . Six issues per year.

Journal of Applied Rehabilitation Counseling. National Rehabilitation Association, 1522 K St., N.W., Washington, DC 20005. 1970- . Quarterly.

Journal of Rehabilitation. National Rehabilitation Association, 1522 K St., N.W., Washington, DC 20005. 1935- . Bimonthly.

Journal of Visual Impairment and Blindness. American Foundation for the Blind, 15 W. 16th St., New York, NY 10011. 1907- . Monthly.

Rehabilitation Counseling Bulletin. American Personnel and Guidance Association, 1607 New Hampshire Ave., N.W., Washington, DC 20009. 1956- . Quarterly.

Rehabilitation Psychology. Rehabilitation Psychology, P.O. Box 26034, Tempe, AZ 85282. 1953- . Quarterly.

Sightsaving Review. National Society to Prevent Blindness, 79 Madison Ave., New York, NY 10016. 1931- . Quarterly.

Sexuality

Archives of Sexual Behavior. Plenum Publishing, 227 W. 17th St.,
New York, NY 10011. 1971- . Six issues per year.

Journal of Homosexuality. Haworth Press, 149 Fifth Ave., New
York, NY 10010. 1974- . Quarterly.

Journal of Sex Research. Society for the Scientific Study of Sex,
138 E. 94th St., New York, NY 10028. 1965- . Quarterly.

Sexuality and Disability. Human Sciences Press, 72 Fifth Ave.,
New York, NY 10011. 1978- . Quarterly.

Social Sciences

Behavioral & Social Sciences Librarian. Haworth Press, 149 Fifth
Ave., New York, NY 10010. 1979- . Quarterly.

Daedalus. American Academy of Arts and Sciences, 165 Allendale
St., Jamaica Plains Sta., Boston, MA 02130. 1958- . Quarterly.

Human Relations: A Journal of Studies Toward the Integration of the
Social Sciences. Plenum Publishing, 227 W. 17th St., New York,
NY 10011. 1947- . Monthly.

Journal of Black Studies. Sage Publications, 275 S. Beverly Dr.,
Beverly Hills, CA 90212. 1970- . Quarterly.

Society: Social Science & Modern Society. Transaction Periodicals
Consortium, Rutgers University, New Brunswick, NJ 08903.
1963- . Bimonthly.

Social Issues and Policy

Journal of Social Issues. Society for the Psychological Study of Social Issues, P.O. Box 1248, Ann Arbor, MI 48106. 1944- .
Quarterly.

Journal of Social Policy. Cambridge University Press, 32 E. 57th
St., New York, NY 10022. 1972- . Quarterly.

Public Interest. National Affairs, P.O. Box 542, Old Chelsea Post
Office, New York, NY 10011. 1965- . Quarterly.

Social Forces. University of North Carolina Press, P.O. Box 2288,
Chapel Hill, NC 27514. 1922- . Quarterly.

Social Problems. Society for Study of Social Problems, 208 Rodwell
Hall, State University of New York, 1300 Elmwood Ave., Buffalo,
NY 14222. 1953- . Five issues per year.

Social Thought. National Conference of Catholic Charities, Suite 307, 1346 Connecticut Ave., N.W., Washington, DC 20036. 1975- . Quarterly.

Urban Affairs Quarterly. Sage Publications, 275 S. Beverly Dr., Beverly Hills, CA 90212. 1965- . Quarterly.

Urban and Social Change Review. Boston College, Graduate School of Social Work, McGuinn Hall, RM 202, Chestnut Hill, MA 02167. 1967- . Biannual.

Social Work--General

Arete: Journal of the College of Social Work, The University of South Carolina. University of South Carolina, Graduate School of Social Work, Columbia, SC 29208. 1970- . Semiannual.

Australian Social Work. Australian Association of Social Workers, P.O. Box 1059, North Richmond, Victoria 3121, Australia. 1947- . Quarterly.

British Journal of Social Work. Academic Press, 111 Fifth Ave., New York, NY 10003. 1971- . Quarterly.

C/O: Journal of Alternative Human Services. Community Congress of San Diego, 1172 Morena Blvd., San Diego, CA 92110. 1974- . Quarterly.

Canadian Journal of Social Work Education/Revue Canadienne d'Education en Servie Social. Canadian Association of Schools of Social Work, Suite 909, 151 Slater St., Ottawa, Ontario K1P5H3, Canada. 1974- . Three issues per year.

Charities U.S.A. National Conference of Catholic Charities, 1346 Connecticut Ave., N.W., Washington, DC 20036. 1974- . Ten issues per year.

Clinical Social Work Journal. Human Sciences Press, 72 Fifth Ave., New York, NY 10011. 1973- . Quarterly.

Community Focus. United Way of America, 801 N. Fairfax, Alexandria, VA 22313. 1977- . Monthly. (Formerly Community.)

Current Information Service: In-Depth Reports. Mental Health Materials Center, 419 Park Ave. S., New York, NY 10016. 1969- . Quarterly.

Disasters. Pergamon Press, Maxwell House, Fairview Park, Elmsford, NY 10523. 1977- . Quarterly.

Health and Social Work. National Association for Social Workers,
Two Park Avenue, New York, NY 10016. 1976- . Quarterly.

Indian Journal of Social Work. Tata Institute of Social Sciences,
Sion-Trombay Rd., Deonar, Bombay 400088, India. 1940- .
Quarterly.

International Social Security Review. International Social Security
Association, P.O. Box 1, 1211 Geneva 22, Switzerland. 1950- .
Quarterly.

International Social Work. International Council on Social Welfare,
Regional Office for Asia and Western Pacific, 175 Daddabbai Nao-
roji Rd., Bombay 40001, India. 1958- . Quarterly.

Journal of Housing. National Association of Housing and Redevelop-
ment Officials, 2600 Virginia Ave., N.W., Washington, DC 20037.
1944- . Monthly.

Journal of Human Resources: Education, Manpower and Welfare
Policies. University of Wisconsin Press, P.O. Box 1379, Madison, WI 53701. 1966- . Quarterly.

Journal of Pastoral Care. Association for Clinical Pastoral Education, Suite 450, 475 Riverside Dr., New York, NY 10027. 1948- .
Quarterly.

Journal of School Social Work. Journal of School Social Work, P.O.
Box 3496, Linden, NJ 07036. 1974- . Quarterly.

Journal of Social Service Research. Haworth Press, 149 Fifth Ave.,
New York, NY 10010. 1977- . Quarterly.

Journal of Social Welfare. University of Kansas, School of Social
Welfare, University of Kansas Press, Lawrence, KS 66045. 1974- .
Two issues per year.

Journal of Sociology and Social Welfare. University of Connecticut,
School of Social Work, 1800 Asylum Ave., West Hartford, CT
06117. 1973- . Bimonthly.

New Human Services Review. Human Sciences Press, 72 Fifth Ave.,
New York, NY 10011. 1974- . Bimonthly.

Perception. Canadian Council on Social Development, 55 Parkdale
Ave., Sta. C, Ottawa, ONT K1Y4G1, Canada. 1924- . Six
issues per year.

Philanthropic Digest. Brakeley, John Price Jones, 1100 17th St.,
N.W., Washington, DC 20036. 1955- . Every three weeks.

Practice Digest. National Association of Social Workers, Two Park
Ave., New York, NY 10016. 1978- . Quarterly.

Public Welfare. American Public Welfare Association, Suite 201, 1155 16th St., N.W., Washington, DC 20036. 1943- . Quarterly.

Smith College Studies in Social Work. Smith College, School for Social Work, Northhampton, MA 01060. 1930- . Three issues per year.

Social Casework. Family Service Association of America, 44 E. 23rd St., New York, NY 10010. 1920- . Monthly, except August and September.

Social Development Issues. University of Iowa, School of Social Work, Iowa City, IA 52242. 1977- . Three issues per year.

Social Security Bulletin. U.S. Social Security Administration, 6401 Security Blvd., Baltimore, MD 21235. 1938- . Monthly.

Social Service Outlook. New York Department of Social Services, 112 State St., Albany, NY 12201. 1966- . Monthly, except July and August.

Social Service Review. University of Chicago Press, 11030 Langley Ave., Chicago, IL 60628. 1927- . Quarterly.

Social Work. National Association of Social Workers, Two Park Ave., New York, NY 10016. 1956- . Bimonthly.

Social Work Education Reporter. Council on Social Work Education, 111 Eighth Ave., New York, NY 10011. 1952- . 3 issues per year.

Social Work Today. British Association of Social Workers, 16 Kent St., Birmingham, 1356RD, England. 1970- . Weekly.

Social Work with Groups. Haworth Press, 149 Fifth Ave., New York, NY 10010. 1978- . Quarterly.

Washington Report. American Public Welfare Association, 1125 15th St., N.W., Washington, DC 20036. 1966- . Ten issues per year.

Washington Social Legislation Bulletin. Child Welfare League of America Social Legislation Information Service, 1346 Connecticut Ave., N.W., Washington, DC 20031. 1944- . Semimonthly.

Sociology

American Journal of Sociology. University of Chicago Press, 5801 Ellis Ave., Chicago, IL 60637. 1895- . Bimonthly.

American Sociological Review. American Sociological Association, 1722 N St., N. W., Washington, DC 20036. 1936- . Bimonthly.

American Sociologist. American Sociologist Association, 1722 N
St., N.W., Washington, DC 20036. 1965- . Quarterly.

Current Anthropology: World Journal of the Sciences of Man. University of Chicago Press, 5801 Ellis Ave., Chicago, IL 60637.
1960- . Quarterly.

Demography. Population Association of America, P.O. Box 1418-2,
B. Franklin Sta., Washington, DC 20044. 1964- . Quarterly.

Journal of Health and Social Behavior. American Sociological Association, 1722 N St., N.W., Washington, DC 20036. 1960- .
Quarterly.

Pacific Sociological Review. Sage Publications, 275 S. Beverly Dr.,
Beverly Hills, CA 90212. 1958- . Quarterly.

Rural Sociology: Devoted to Scientific Study of Rural and Small Town
Life. Rural Sociological Society, Texas A & M University, College Station, TX 77843. 1936- . Quarterly.

Sociological Quarterly. Midwest Sociological Society, Department of
Sociology, Southern Illinois University, Carbondale, IL 62901.
1960- . Quarterly.

Sociological Symposium. Virginia Polytechnic Institute and State University, Dept. of Sociology, Blacksbury, VA 24061. 1968- .
Quarterly.

Sociology & Social Research: An International Journal. University
of Southern California, Los Angeles, CA 90007. 1916- . Quarterly.

Sociometry: A Journal of Research in Social Psychology. American
Sociological Association, 1722 N St., N.W., Washington, DC
20044. 1937- . Quarterly.

B. SOCIAL SERVICE ORGANIZATIONS

Alcohol and Drug Problems Association of North America
1130 17th St., N.W.
Washington, DC   20036
(202) 452-0990

American Academy of Pediatrics
1801 Hinman Ave.
Evanston, IL   60204
(312) 869-4255

American Association for Marriage and Family Therapy

924 W. Ninth
Upland, CA 91786
(714) 981-0888

American Association of Homes for the Aged
1050 17th St., N.W.
Washington, DC 20036
(202) 296-5960

American Association of Suicidology
Central Office
2459 S. Ash
Denver, CO 80222

American Catholic Correctional Chaplains Association
Federal Correctional Institution
Anthony, NM 88021
(915) 886-3422

American Foundation for the Blind
15 W. 16th St.
New York, NY 10011
(212) 620-2000

American Hospital Association
840 N. Lake Shore Dr.
Chicago, IL 60611
(312) 280-6000

American Humane Association
5351 S. Roslyn St.
Englewood, CO 80111

American Medical Association
535 N. Dearborn St.
Chicago, IL 60610
(312) 751-6000

American Occupational Therapy Association
6000 Executive Blvd., Suite 200
Rockville, MD 20852
(301) 770-2200

American Psychiatric Association
1700 18th St., N.W.
Washington, DC 20009
(202) 797-4900

American Psychological Association
1200 17th St., N.W.
Washington, DC 20036
(202) 833-7600

American Public Welfare Association
1155 16th St., N.W., Suite 201
Washington, DC 20036
(202) 293-7550

American Red Cross
17th and D St., N.W.
Washington, DC 20006
(202) 737-8300

Association of Jewish Family and Children's Agencies
200 Park Ave. S., 6th Fl.
New York, NY 10003
(212) 674-6659

Child Welfare League of America
67 Irving Place
New York, NY 10003
(212) 254-7410

Children's Defense Fund
1520 New Hampshire Ave., N.W.
Washington, DC 20036
(202) 483-1470

Coalition for Children and Youth
815 Fifteenth St., N.W.
Washington, DC 20005
(202) 347-9386

Consumer Protection Center
2000 H St., N. W.
Washington, DC 20052
(202) 676-7585

Council on Social Work Education
345 E. 46th St.
New York, NY 10011
(212) 242-3800

Day Care and Child Development Council of America
1012 14th St., N.W., Suite 1104
Washington, DC 20005
(212) 638-2316

Families Anonymous
P.O. Box 344
Torrance, CA 90501
(213) 775-3211

Family Service Association of America
44 E. 23rd St.
New York, NY 10010
(212) 674-6100

Federation of Protestant Welfare Agencies
281 Park Ave. S.
New York, NY   10010
(212) 777-4800

International Association of Schools of Social Work
Freytaggasse 32
A-1210 Vienna, Austria

International Halfway House Association
2525 Victory Pkwy., Suite 101
Cincinnati, OH   45206
(513) 221-3250

International Institute of Stress
659 Milton St.
Montreal, PQ, Canada   H2XLW6
(514) 343-6665

National Assembly of National Voluntary Health and Social Welfare
    Organizations
291 Broadway
New York, NY   10007
(212) 267-1700

National Association for Community Development
1424 16th St., N.W., Room 106
Washington, DC   20036
(202) 833-9280

National Association of Christians in Social Work
P.O. Box 84
Wheaton, IL   60184

National Association of Private Residential Facilities for the Mentally
    Retarded
6269 Leesburg Pike, Suite B-5
Falls Church, VA   22044
(703) 536-3311

National Center on Child Abuse and Neglect
Administration for Children, Youth and Families
P.O. Box 1182
Washington, DC   20013
(202) 755-0587

National Coalition of Hispanic Mental Health
1015 15th St., N.W., Suite 402
Washington, DC   20005
(202) 638-0505

National Committee for Prevention of Child Abuse
111 East Wacker Dr., Room 510
Chicago, IL   60604
(312) 565-1100

National Conference of Catholic Charities
1346 Connecticut Ave. , N.W.
Washington, DC   20036
(202) 785-2757

National Council of Churches
475 Riverside Dr. , Room 576
New York, NY   10027
(212) 870-2200

National Council of Senior Citizens
1511 K St. , N.W.
Washington, DC   20005
(202) 347-8800

National Council on Alcoholism
733 Third Avenue
New York, NY   10017
(212) 986-4433

National Council on Crime and Delinquency
411 Hackensack Ave.
Hackensack, NJ   07601
(201) 488-0400

National Council on the Aging
1828 L St. , N.W.
Washington, DC   20036
(202) 223-6250

National Federation of Settlements and Neighborhood Centers
232 Madison Ave.
New York, NY   10016
(212) 679-6110

National Home Caring Council
67 Irving Place
New York, NY   10003
(212) 674-4990

National Legal Aid and Defender Association
1625 K St. , N.W.
Washington, DC   20006
(202) 452-0620

National Self-Help Clearinghouse
33 W. 42nd St. , Room 1227
New York, NY   10036
(212) 840-7606

National Society for Austistic Children
1234 Massachusetts Ave. , N.W. , Suite 1017
Washington, DC   20005
(202) 783-0125

National Urban Coalition
1201 Connecticut Ave. , N.W.
Washington, DC   20036
(202) 331-2400

National Urban League
500 E. 62nd St.
New York, NY   10021
(212) 644-6500

National Youth Alternatives Project
1830 Connecticut Ave. , N.W.
Washington, DC   20009
(202) 785-0764

Planned Parenthood Federation
810 Seventh Ave.
New York, NY   10019
(212) 541-7800

Rape Crisis Center
P.O. Box 21005
Washington, DC   20009
(202) 333-7273

Regional Institute of Social Welfare Research
P.O. Box 152
Athens, GA   30603
(404) 542-7614

Retarded Infant Services
386 Park Ave. S.
New York, NY   10016
(212) 582-1128

United Way of America
801 N. Fairfax St.
Alexandria, VA   22314
(703) 836-7100

C.   SOCIAL WORK LIBRARIES

GENERAL

<u>Alabama</u>

Alabama State Department of Pensions and Security Library
64 N. Union St.
Administration Bldg. , Room 507
Montgomery, AL   36130
(205) 832-5916

Arizona

Division of Behavioral Health Services Library
Arizona State Department of Health Services
2500 E. Van Buren
Phoenix, AZ 85008
(602) 244-1331

California

Social Welfare Library
University of California
216 Haviland Hall
Berkeley, CA 94720
(415) 642-4432

United Way, Inc. , Library
621 S. Virgil Ave.
Los Angeles, CA 90005
(213) 380-1450

Social Work Library
University of Southern California
University Park
Los Angeles, CA 90302
(213) 743-7932

Elftman Memorial Library
Salvation Army School for Officers Training
30840 Hawthorne Blvd.
Rancho Palos Verdes, CA 90274

Colorado

Colorado State Department of Social Service Library
1575 Sherman St.
Denver, CO 80203
(303) 839-2251

Medical Library
Fort Logan Mental Health Center
3520 W. Oxford Ave.
Denver, CO 80236
(303) 761-0220

Connecticut

School of Social Work Library
University of Connecticut
Greater Hartford Campus

West Hartford, CT 06117
(203) 523-4841

District of Columbia

Department Library
U. S. Department of Health and Human Services
330 Independence Ave. , S. E. , Room 1436 N.
Washington, DC 20003
(202) 245-6339

National Association of Social Workers Resource Center
1425 H St. , N. W. , No. 600
Washington, DC 20005
(202) 628-6800

Florida

Audio Visual Section
Florida State Department of Health and Rehabilitative Services
1217 Pearl St.
Jacksonville, FL 32231

Resource Center
Florida State Department of Health and Rehabilitative Services
1317 Winewood Blvd. , Bldg. 2, Room 118
Tallahassee, FL 32301
(904) 487-2312

Georgia

Addison M. Duval Library
Georgia Mental Health Institute
Georgia State Department of Human Resources
1256 Briar Rd. N. E.
Atlanta, GA 30306
(404) 894-5663

Illinois

Resource Center
Chicago Department of Human Resources
640 N. LaSalle St.
Chicago, IL 60610
(312) 744-4043

Social Service Administration Library
University of Chicago
969 E. 60th St.

Chicago, IL 60637
(312) 753-3426

United Charities of Chicago Library
64 E. Jackson Blvd.
Chicago, IL 60604
(312) 939-5930

Indiana

Medical Library
Carter Memorial Hospital
1315 W. 10th St.
Indianapolis, IN 46202
(317) 634-8401

Iowa

Iowa State Department of Social Services Library
Hoover Bldg.
Des Moines, IA 50319
(515) 281-5925

Kansas

Staff Development Training Center Library
Kansas State Department of Social and Rehabilitation Services
2700 W. Sixth St.
Topeka, KS 66606
(913) 296-4327

Kentucky

Kentucky State Department for Human Resources Library
275 E. Main St.
Frankfort, KY 40601
(502) 564-4530

Maine

Departmental Library
Maine State Department of Human Resources
State House
Augusta, ME 04333
(207) 289-3055

Research Center Library
Center for Research and Advanced Study

246 Deering Ave.
Portland, ME   04102

Maryland

Staff Reference Library
Health and Welfare Council of Central Maryland
22 Light St.
Baltimore, MD   21202
(301) 752-4146

U. S. Social Security Administration Library
Altmeyer Bldg. , Room 570
6401 Security Blvd.
Baltimore, MD   21235

Massachusetts

School of Social Work Library
Simmons College
51 Commonwealth Ave.
Boston, MA   02115
(617) 266-0806

Graduate School of Social Work Library
Boston College
McGuinn Hall
Chestnut Hill, MA   02167
(617) 969-0100

Michigan

Social Work Library
University of Michigan
1548 Frieze Bldg.
Ann Arbor, MI   48109
(313) 764-5169

Sociology and Economic Department
Detroit Public Library
5201 Woodward Ave.
Detroit, MI   48202
(313) 833-1440

Minnesota

Social Welfare History Archives
Wilson Library
University of Minnesota

309 19th Ave. S.
Minneapolis, MN   55455
(612) 373-4420

Minnesota State Department of Public Welfare Library
Centennial Bldg. , 1st Floor
St. Paul, MN   55155
(612) 296-1548

Mississippi

Jean Gunter Social Welfare Library
Mississippi State Department of Public Welfare
Dale Bldg. , 2906 N. State St.
Jackson, MS   39216
(601) 981-7080

Missouri

Library and Learning Resources Center
George Warren Brown School of Social Work
Washington University
Box 1196
St. Louis, MO   63130
(314) 889-6616

Nebraska

Nebraska State Department of Public Welfare
301 Centennial Mall S. , 5th Floor
Lincoln, NE   68508
(402) 471-3121

New Jersey

Monmouth County Social Services Library
Box 3000
Freehold, NJ   07728
(201) 431-6011

New York

Adelphi University Social Work Library
Adelphi University
Garden City, NY   11530
(516) 294-8700

Center on Social Welfare Policy and Law Library
95 Madison Ave. , Room 707

New York, NY   10016
(212) 679-3709

Family Service Association of America Library
44 E. 23rd St.
New York, NY   10010
(212) 674-6100

Hunter College School of Social Work Library
Hunter College of the City University of New York
129 E. 79th St.
New York, NY   10021
(212) 360-2646

Institute of Public Administration Library
55 W. 44th St.
New York, NY   10036
(212) 730-5632

Jacob Alson Memorial Library
Anti-Defamation League of B'nai B'rith
823 United Nations Plaza
New York, NY   10017
(212) 689-7400

Landowne-Bloom Library
Yeshiva University
55 Fifth Ave., 12th Floor
New York, NY   10003
(212) 790-0236

Library at Lincoln Center
Fordham University
Leon Lowenstein Bldg.
New York, NY   10023
(212) 841-5130

M. C. Magel Memorial Library
American Foundation for the Blind
15 W. 16th St.
New York, NY   10011
(212) 924-0420

McMillan Library
New York City Human Resources Administration
109 E. 16th St.
New York, NY   10003
(212) 460-8555

YMCA Historical Library
National Council of the Young Men's Christian Association of the U. S.
291 Broadway
New York, NY 10007
(212) 374-2042

Whitney M. Young Jr. Memorial Library of Social Work
Columbia University
309 International Affairs Bldg.
New York, NY 10027
(212) 280-5159

Brengle Memorial Library
Salvation Army School for Officers Training
201 Lafeyette Ave.
Suffern, NY 10901
(914) 357-3500

Ohio

Applied Social Sciences Library
School of Applied Social Science
Case Western Reserve University
2034 Abington Rd.
Cleveland, OH 44106
(216) 368-2302

Social Work Library
Ohio State University
1947 College Rd.
Columbus, OH 43210
(614) 422-6627

Pennsylvania

School of Social Administration Library
Temple University
565 Ritter Hall Annex
Philadelphia, PA 19122
(215) 787-1209

Smalley Library of Social Work
School of Social Work
University of Pennsylvania
3701 Locust Walk
Philadelphia, PA 19104
(215) 243-5508

Action-House Library
2 Gateway Ctr.
Pittsburgh, PA 15222
(412) 281-2102

School of Social Work Library
University of Pittsburgh
Pittsburgh, PA 15260
(412) 624-4456

Rhode Island

Staff Development Library
Rhode Island Staff Department of Social and Rehabilitative
Services
600 New London Ave.
Cranston, RI 02920
(401) 464-3111

Tennessee

Tennessee State Department of Human Services
111 Seventh Ave N.
Nashville, TN 37203

Texas

Abilene State School Library
Box 451
Abilene, TX 79604
(915) 692-4054

Texas State Department of Human Resources
P. O. Box 2960
Austin, TX 78769
(512) 458-8568

Worden School of Social Service Library
Our Lady of the Lake University
411 S. W. 24th St.
San Antonio, TX 76285
(512) 434-6711

Utah

Social Work Library
University of Utah
Social Work Bldg.
Salt Lake City, UT 84112
(801) 581-8177

Virginia

Information Center
United Way of America
801 N. Fairfax St.
Alexandria, VA 22314
(703) 836-7100

Washington

Social Work Library
University of Washington
JG-14
Seattle, WA 98195
(206) 543-5742

Wisconsin

Research and Instructional Media Center
School of Social Work
University of Wisconsin
425 Henry Mall, Room 163
Madison, WI 53706
(608) 263-3663

Virginia L. Franks Memorial Library
School of Social Work
University of Wisconsin
425 Henry Mall, Room 230
Madison, WI 53706
(608) 263-3840

Catholic Social Services Library
206 E. Michigan St.
Milwaukee, WI 53202
(414) 271-2881

Research Library
Milwaukee County Board of Supervisors
901 N. Ninth St., Room 201
Milwaukee, WI 53233
(414) 278-4952

AGING

California

Ethel Percy Andrus Gerontology Center
University of Southern California
3715 McClintock Ave.
Los Angeles, CA 90007
(212) 743-5990

District of Columbia

Gerontology Resource Center
National Retired Teachers Association--American Association of
   Retired Persons

1909 K St., N.W.
Washington, DC 20049
(202) 872-4845

National Council on the Aging Library
1828 L St., N.W.
Washington, DC 20036
(202) 223-6250

Maryland

National Institute on Aging
4940 Eastern Ave.
Baltimore, MD 21224
(301) 396-9403

Michigan

Learning Resource Center
Institute of Gerontology
University of Michigan
520 E. Library St.
Ann Arbor, MI 48109
(313) 763-1325

Gerontology Learning Resources Center
Institute of Gerontology
Wayne State University
203 Library Ct.
Detroit, MI 48202
(313) 577-2221

Ohio

Scripps Foundation for Research in Population Problems and Geron-
tology Center
Miami University
Hoyt Library
Oxford, OH 45056
(513) 529-2914

Oregon

Resource Center
Oregon Center for Gerontology at the University of Oregon
1627 Agate St.
Eugene, OR 97403
(503) 686-4207

DELINQUENCY

District of Columbia

National Institute of Justice Library
U.S. Department of Justice
633 Indiana Ave., N.W.
Washington, DC   20531
(301) 492-9149

Nebraska

Boys Town Library Services Division
Center for the Study of Youth Development
Boys Town, NE   68010
(402) 498-1420

New Jersey

National Council on Crime and Delinquency Library
Continental Plaza
411 Hackensack Ave.
Hackensack, NJ   07601
(201) 488-0400

North Carolina

Learning Resource Center
North Carolina State Justice Academy
Drawer 99
Salemburg, NC   28385
(919) 525-4151

DRUG AND ALCOHOL ABUSE

District of Columbia

U.S. Drug Enforcement Administration Library
1405 I Street, N.W.
Washington, DC   20537
(202) 633-1369

Illinois

Central State Institute of Addictions Library
120 W. Huron St.
Chicago, IL   60610

Maryland

Resource Center
National Clearinghouse for Drug Abuse Information
Box 416
Kensington, MD   20795
(301) 443-6500

National Clearinghouse for Alcohol Information Library
Box 2345
Rockville, MD   21044
(301) 468-2600

Minnesota

Drug Information Service Center
University of Minnesota
32 Appleby Hall
128 Pleasant St.
Minneapolis, MN   55455

Texas

Drug Abuse Council Library
Drug Abuse Epidemiology Data Center
Institute of Behavioral Research
Texas Christian University
Fort Worth, TX   76129
(817) 921-7674

FAMILY PLANNING

Maryland

National Clearinghouse for Family Planning Information
Box 2225
Rockville, MD   20852
(301) 881-9400

HANDICAPPED

District of Columbia

National Clearinghouse Library
U. S. Commission on Civil Rights
1121 Vermont Ave. , N.W.
Washington, DC   20005
(202) 254-6636

Illinois

Information Center
National Easter Seal Society for Crippled Children and Adults
2023 W. Ogden Ave.
Chicago, IL   60612
(312) 243-8400

Virginia

CEC Information Services
ERIC Clearinghouse on Handicapped and Gifted Children
Council for Exceptional Children
1920 Association Dr.
Reston, VA   22091
(703) 620-3660

MENTAL HEALTH

Maryland

Mental Health Study Center Library
National Institute of Mental Health
U. S. Public Health Service
2340 University Blvd. , E.
Adelphi, MD   20783
(301) 436-6340

Communication Center
National Institute of Mental Health
U. S. Public Health Service
Park Lawn Bldg. , Room 15 C-OS
5600 Fishers Lane
Rockville, MD   20857
(301) 443-4507

National Clearinghouse for Mental Health Information
5600 Fishers Lane, Room 11 A 31
Rockville, MD   20857
(301) 443-4517

POVERTY

California

Western Center on Law and Poverty Library
3535 W. Sixth St.
Los Angeles, CA   90020
(213) 487-7211

District of Columbia

Action Library
Action
806 Connecticut Ave. , N. W.
Washington, DC   20525
(202) 254-3307

Community Services Administration Library
1200 19th St. , N. W.
Washington, DC   20506
(202) 254-5756

Minnesota

Minnesota State Office of Economic Opportunity Library
690 American Center Bldg.
St. Paul, MN   55101
(612) 296-8810

New Jersey

Center for Urban Policy Research Library
Rutgers University
Kilmer Area Bldg. 4051
Piscataway, NJ   08854
(201) 932-3136

New York

New York City Human Resources Administration Library
109 E. 16th St.
New York, NY   10003
(212) 460-8555

Wisconsin

Gerald G. Somers Graduate Reference Room
University of Wisconsin
8432 Social Sciences Bldg.
1180 Observatory Drive
Madison, WI   53706
(608) 262-6195

AUTHOR INDEX

Abraham, Samuel V. 134
Abrams, Charles 182
Addams, Jane 77
Advisory Board on Child Abuse and Neglect 255
Alcohol and Drug Problems Association of North America 236
Aldous, Joan 367, 368
Alexander, Shana 552
Allen, Robert D. 504
Allyn, Mildred V. 195
Alperin, Melvin 508
Alperin, Stanley 508
Amary, Issam B. 501
American Academy of Pediatrics 301, 311
American Association of Homes for the Aging 207, 218, 219
American Association of Marriage and Family Counselors 391
American Association of Suicidology 538
American Correctional Association 322
American Foundation for the Blind 416, 428, 434, 436
American Hospital Association 448, 463, 473, 474, 475, 479
American Humane Association 288
American Psychiatric Association 107
American Public Welfare Association 50, 190, 523
Ammer, Christine 135
Ammer, Dean S. 135
Annas, George J. 464, 599
Areen, Judith 299, 327
Arieti, Silvano 117

Arnada, Paul 348
Astin, Helen S. 526
Atkins, Jacqueline Marx 403
Austin, Gregory A. 222
Axinn, June 78

Baer, Betty L. 651, 652
Balkema, John B. 196
Ballou, Patricia K. 541
Barkas, J. L. 32
Baskin, Barbara Holland 412
Bauman, Mary K. 413
Baxter, James W. 493
Beere, Carol A. 553
Bell, Duran 197, 332
Bell, Gwendolyn 171
Belli, Donna 353
Bendick, Marc, Jr. 521
Bennett, Alwina 435
Benson, Hazel B. 260
Berlin, Irving N. 261
Bernstein, Joanne E. 262
Berryman, Phillip 582
Biegel, Leonard 213
Blank, Marion S. 370
Bludworth, Edward 239
Boatner, Maxine T. 425
Boguslawski, Dorothy Beers 305
Bommarito, James W. 289
Boston, Guy 315, 593
Boston Women's Collective 550
Boyce, Byrl N. 172, 334
Brantley, James R. 316
Bravieri, Joanne 244
Bremner, Robert H. 79, 80, 81, 82, 83
Brennan, Jere L. 335
Breul, Frank R. 84
Brewer, Joan Scherer 527
Brian, J. L. Berry 184